TARGET GOLF

Lower Scores by "Visualizing" Your Game

Roy Pace
with Al Barkow
Foreword by J. C. Snead

THE BODY
PRESS

ABOUT THE AUTHOR

Roy Pace is a former PGA touring pro who is now head pro at the Wee Burn Country Club in Darien, CT. As a teacher, Roy has received numerous PGA awards and is a member of the Texas' Pro's Hall of Fame.

Published by The Body Press, a division of HPBooks, Inc.
P.O. Box 5367, Tucson, AZ 85703   602/888-2150
ISBN: 0-89586-354-5   Library of Congress Catalog No. 85-73184

Publisher
Rick Bailey

Editorial Director
Theodore DiSante

Art Director
Don Burton

Book Design
Paul Fitzgerald

Typography
Cindy Coatsworth
Michelle Carter

Director of Manufacturing
Anthony B. Narducci

Photography
Barbara Nitke

Acknowledgement
Cover photographed at
Tucson National Golf Club
and Spa with the kind
assistance of Sherry Cross.

Material prepared by
Rudledge Books, a division
of Sammis Publishing
Corporation, 122 E. 25th
St., New York, NY 10010

Contents

Foreword

I met Roy Pace in Bogota, Columbia in 1968, when we were playing the Caribbean Tour. I was a rookie on the tour then, and really needed a friend. That's where Roy came in. He had been a tour regular for about eight years and well-known as a player with a lot of talent and an impressive knowledge of the game of golf. Soon after we met, we practiced together and worked diligently on swing mechanics.

Then, as now, Roy's great teaching ability was obvious. I have always thought that the best golf teachers are those who have played professionally or have had a great deal of competitive experience. They know which swings and techniques will work under pressure, because they have used them in pressure situations.

That's the foundation of Roy's instruction, and I'm convinced that the principles described and illustrated in this book will give you the high-performance results you want.

J. C. Snead
Hot Springs, VA

Introduction

As the subtitle of this book suggests, I stress the *target game* of golf. Target golf means more than you might expect. We'll be talking about hitting the ball into a *particular part* of the fairway, for example, not just into the rough grass. Or, "targeting" a specific spot on the green and, once on the green, targeting to get the ball into the hole, not just close to the pin.

All of this may seem obvious, but most weekend golfers don't pay enough attention to it. Instead, they concern themselves primarily with hitting the ball. As a result, they don't play as well as they could.

I know what you're thinking:

- "But don't you have to know *how* to hit the ball before you can think about *where* you want to hit it?"
- "Isn't hitting the ball well objective number one?"

IF YOU ARE A BEGINNER

These points are well taken and, for the beginner, the fundamentals of grip, stance, and swing are most important. And for those of you just starting to play golf we talk about these fundamentals. But in my experience as a teaching pro, I've found that it doesn't take very long for beginning golfers to get the general feel of the game. They soon start asking about ways to lower their scores—which means making better shots. That's where the target game comes in.

IF YOU PLAY GOLF ALREADY

For you readers with some golfing experience, this book features a reintroduction to the fundamentals. Don't be bored by what appears to be a rehash of what you already know. I strongly urge you to read what I have to say. Who knows? You may find a tip or two that will improve your game right away. For example a new technique I stress is to release the hands in the downswing. Mastering that can help *any* player.

In this book I show you how to combine the fundamentals of golf with the mental aspects of target golf.

THE TARGET GAME IN BRIEF

We humans have a peculiar quirk. We perform fairly complex physical actions better when we think more about the end than the means. For example, all golfers have had the experience of hitting a very good shot and realizing that they seemed to do it without conscious effort.

Say you need to hit the ball over a water hazard onto a green. You choose a club, set the target in you mind's eye, and swing through the ball. You've done it! It's a beautiful feeling, but why did it all seem so easy? It's simply that you set your target and hit through without distraction. That's the basic tenet of the target game of golf.

There is no denying the sheer pleasure that comes from hitting a golf ball well—the power, the take-off, the sight of the ball sailing through the air. What I will be emphasizing here is that you will hit better shots when you think less about the mechanics!

Playing vs. Hitting—If you think only of hitting the ball and not where you want it to go, you are not really *playing* golf. Rather, you are *hitting* golf. When you pay more attention to targeting the ball, hitting with the purpose of getting it to a certain place, you are *playing* golf. Because you will hit more good shots playing golf, you end up killing two birds with one stone—you get more sporting thrills *and* you produce lower scores.

FOCUSING

To play target golf, you must "narrow your vision." Everyone understands that the ball should be hit into the fairway with a drive off the tee. But the fairway is relatively wide. To really get the benefit of target golf you should aim for a certain part of the fairway—left, right or center.

You'll learn to "target" all of your shots from the tee to the green. Without a doubt, you'll soon be playing (not hitting) better golf.

This kind of "focusing" has the same effect as looking through a camera. The viewfinder cuts off peripheral vision. You don't see anything to the sides of your subject. This is especially important in golf, because you can get into trouble with stray shots to the sides. Hone your vision to concentrate on a 10-yard-wide area of the fairway, or a particular side of the green, and "ignore" the rough, trees, bunkers, or water hazards that may be mere yards away.

Concentrating on precisely where you want to put the ball produces a positive approach to playing the game. Because there are so many obvious hazards on a golf course, it is natural to have them in the forefront of your mind as you consider a shot and prepare to play it. Playing target golf helps you exclude these distractions.

If your last thought before hitting the ball is on the sand trap or pond you are trying to avoid, the odds are that you will hit the ball into trouble. If, however, your last thought before swinging is a target area on the green, you have a much better chance of ending up there. Thinking *sand trap* or *pond* is negative golf. Thinking *green* is positive, target golf.

In a situation like this, simply visualizing and thinking "target" during the shot will help get you there.

If you learn nothing else from this book, learn to use a target on *every* shot. Just this one lesson alone can greatly improve a golfer's game.

USING EXPERTS

Pay close attention to the photographs in this book, especially if you are a beginner. Imitate the motions illustrated. You can probably learn as much about swinging a golf club from watching and mimicking as from reading the text. For the same reason, I urge you to watch expert golfers in action. It's possible to pick up ideas on swing mechanics and golfing techniques.

Perhaps most important, you will learn from them a sense of rhythm and tempo. You will find that good golfers, regardless of the shape of their swings, will generally not force shots. Their swings are balanced and rhythmic, two things all golfers should strive for.

A common observation among beginning athletes is that the experts make everything "look so easy." They do, but it's not necessarily because they have special gifts. In golf it's generally because *they don't force the swing.* They make it look easy because they aren't swinging too hard.

Be Realistic — The target method is not foolproof. You should accept the fact that you *will* hit some balls into the sand or water — even if your last thought was targeted on the green. Don't let this cause unnecessary frustration. It is impossible to hit every shot perfectly. Even the game's greatest golfers cannot do it.

The difference between the pros and the rest of us is that pros understand that golf is actually a game of misses and near-misses. Only a few shots of any round are made perfectly. The real secret of good golf is to "miss 'em good," as the saying goes. That is, when the ball is mishit, the error is not serious because the ball travels forward and goes reasonably straight. The result is that the ball gets closer to the hole and the next shot is not especially difficult.

Target golf, as you can see, is not guaranteed 100% of the time. Even so, it *will* help you make more good shots—and better misses.

GOLF TIP

Golf balls may vary, not so much by brand name as by type. Solid balls go farther when hit with an iron. Most pros still use the natural-rubber-covered ball. Although it cuts more easily, the ball give more control because it is easier to spin.

CHAPTER ONE

The Grip & Address

The basic fundamental of golf is *the grip*. The *address position*—how you stand at the ball when ready to hit it—is a close second.

Because your hands are the only part of your body in actual contact with the club, a correct grip is essential to playing good golf. A correct grip makes the clubhead seem to be an extension of your hands, and the "feel" in your hands is transmitted to the clubhead through the shaft of the club.

The first thing I look at when I give a lesson is the student's grip. If it is sound, I go on to other things. Over the years I've carefully studied how the greatest players grip the club. They all seem to possess an ability to place their hands in a natural, simple manner so they appear molded to the club grip. The hands molded together act as a single unit, allowing for a free and controlled motion in the swing.

BASIC GRIP AND ADDRESS

In the target game, each shot is aimed at a specific place on the course. The most efficient way to hit the ball where you're aiming is with the clubface at a 90° angle, or *square*, to the target at impact. The grip you use on the club plays a big role in keeping the clubface square to the target.

Basically, you place your hands on the club as though you were shaking hands with it. For a right-handed player, the back of the left hand and the palm of the right hand should directly face the target. This is what I refer to as a *neutral* grip. I will explain that term in a moment when I get into more detail on the grip.

The back of each hand should be square to the clubface.

The address is more complicated than the grip because it involves positioning more body parts. If just one of those positions is incorrect, the effectiveness of your swing will suffer. Essentially, the address influences the path of the club as you swing it. This affects how well and how accurately you hit the ball.

For example, if you persistently hit the ball too high and slice it to the right of your target, you may be tilting your body too much to the right at address. You may get into this position without even realizing it. In addition, you may unwittingly make a grip change for the worse. Without being aware of it, you may, for example, have slightly turned your right hand clockwise. This happens even among excellent players.

How To Adjust—When a pro's game begins to fail him, the first thing he does is check his grip and address. He compares his current grip and address to what he knows to be the fundamentals of those two most important golfing basics. Bit by bit the pro analyzes the grip and address positions, knowing that sometimes only a minor adjustment in either can correct something that has gone awry.

This procedure is something that all golfers should learn how to do. But first you must learn the fundamentals of the grip and address. Then you will always have the basics to check yourself against.

THE GRIP

Although both hands are involved in the grip, each hand has its own job. I will describe the differences, but I want to emphasize that once you understand the differences and they become part of your swing, you must let the hands work together as a single unit.

From here on out, I will assume that you are right-handed. If you are left-handed, mentally switch *left hand* for *right hand* and vice-versa in the following descriptions.

Left-Hand Security—The left hand *holds* the club, maintaining it with firm, but not tight, control. It is the security guard that keeps the club from shifting or moving around in your hands during the swing. The ring and little fingers of your left hand hold the handle of the club most firmly, keeping the club secure during the start (the *takeaway*) and at the top of the backswing.

The club handle should lie between the first and second finger joints of your left hand and should rest at the base of the fourth and little finger. You want the club to feel securely gripped with these last two fingers.

When you close your left hand around the club handle, the heel or pad of your hand should be directly on top of the club. Be careful that the pad of your left hand rests

The handle of the club rests at the base of your fingers. Rest the heel of your hand on top of the shaft. Keep your ring and little fingers firm.

securely on top of the handle. This allows the pad and the index finger to work together to keep the club in balance.

Your left thumb should be slightly to the right of center along the top of the handle. Don't stretch the thumb too far down the handle or bring it up too short. Let it take a comfortable, natural position.

When your left hand is closed around the handle, your fingertips should just barely touch the heel of your hand. If they dig into the heel, the club grip is probably too small and needs building up. If your fingers do not touch the heel of your hand, then the grip is too big for your hand. Any good golf professional or golf-club repairman can adjust the grip to your hand. Having the right size *is* important.

Right-Hand Hitter—The right hand's primary function is to direct the motion of the clubhead in both the backswing and downswing. The right hand has more "feel" of the club than the left. For this reason, you grip relatively lightly with your right hand.

Do not place the club in the palm of your right hand! Many beginning golfers tend to do this, probably because they are right-handed and believe that the right hand gives them power.

Frank Beard, a leading money-winner when he played on the tour, once made a good point to me about the right hand in the golf grip. He noted that if you were going to test the feel of something, such as a piece of cloth, you would grasp the material with the tips of your fingers, because they have greatest sensitivity.

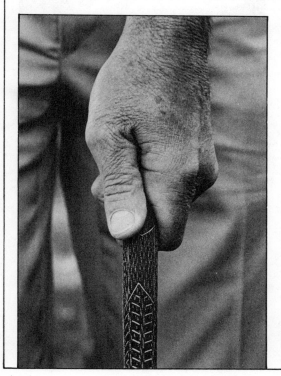

Your left thumb should be comfortable and slightly right of center — at 1:00 as you look down the shaft.

The same applies to holding a golf club with the right hand. You want sensitivity, or "feel," in the right hand. Feel promotes *flexibility*—which means power.

Set the club handle just inside the callus line of your right hand. Your right thumb should angle across the top of the handle from right to left.

I use two checkpoints to make sure that I'm placing the right hand correctly:

1) Snugly cover the left thumb with the palm of the right hand. Try to place the horizontal crease in the middle of your right palm directly over the middle of your left thumb.

2) Form a hook with the index finger of your right hand. This finger should be slightly separated from the other fingers of your hand. The first knuckle of your index finger should rest directly beneath the handle of the club. Imagine that your index finger is in a position to trigger a gun. This hook formed by your index finger gives you the leverage to return the clubhead squarely to the ball at impact.

ESTABLISHING GRIP
1) The crease between the pads in your right hand covers the left thumb.

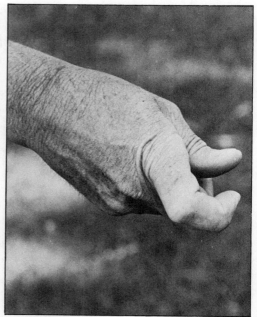

2) The first knuckle of your right index finger rests behind the club handle. The index finger splits away from the other fingers to form a "hook."

GOLF TIP

Here are two ways to read strange greens: If it is a seaside course, the grain will take the ball toward the ocean. If it's in a mountainous area, the ball will roll away from the mountain and toward the setting sun.

3) The end of your right thumb and index finger extend down the club handle equally.

4) The complete grip, showing how your hands should fit together as one unit.

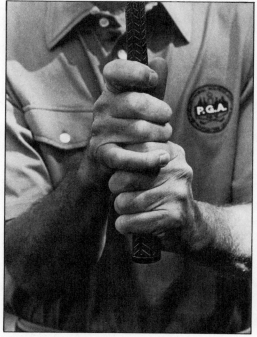

The overlapping grip. You may also hear it called the *Vardon grip.*

The interlocking grip.

Making the Connection—There are two standard methods for connecting the right hand with the left hand and making them perform as a unit. They are the *overlapping* and *interlocking* positions.

I favor the overlapping method because I think it is generally more comfortable—there is less feeling of tightness. But if you have fairly short fingers, you may want to use the interlocking method. That's what Jack Nicklaus uses, so it can't be bad.

To use the overlapping method, place the little finger of your right hand on top of the crevice formed by the index and middle fingers of your left hand.

To use the interlocking grip, intertwine the little finger of your right hand with the index finger of your left.

Checkpoint #1 — Notice how the V formed by the thumb and forefinger of the right hand hits a point between my chin and shoulder. The same is true of the left hand.

Hands Together—When your grip is completely formed, use the following checkpoints to determine if your grip is correct:

1) The V's formed by the thumb and forefinger of each hand should be pointed at your right shoulder. The V's may not be pointed precisely at your right shoulder—depending on the size and shape of your hands, and how much they are rotated—but they shouldn't be too far off.

2) The palms of your hands should be facing each other just as they do when they are hanging at your sides in a normal, relaxed way. To illustrate this point without holding a golf club, swing your hands up from your sides and in front of you as though you were going to take hold of a golf club. Open your hands as you bring them together. The palms will slap against each other. That's essentially how they should correspond to each other when you are gripping a golf club.

Checkpoint #2 — Hands are square to the clubface.

Grip Pressure—It is difficult to prescribe exactly how much pressure you should exert on the club handle. First of all, there is no precise way to gauge how much is best. Every golfer has his or her own strength and confidence. What is tight for one person may be too loose for another.

Some golf instructors teach that the grip pressure should be "as light as a feather." Others think it should be a hard squeeze. An overly tight grip, however, will tense the muscles in your arms and shoulders and cause a loss of flexibility. And a grip that is as "light as a feather" can make you feel insecure about club control.

The best advice I can give you is to achieve a middle ground. Visualize trying to grip a golf club as though you were holding a small bird in your hands. Don't hold it so tight as to hurt it, but not so loose as to let it fly away either. A good tip for finding the correct grip pressure is to squeeze and release the handle a few times. This helps you settle on the pressure that is most comfortable and right for you.

Perhaps even more important than your overall grip pressure is the relative grip pressure of each of your fingers. I strongly recommend, for example, that the last two fingers of your left hand exert a bit more pressure than the others. This helps prevent the club from coming loose at the top of the backswing. If your club separates from your hand at this critical part of the swing, it is usually the last two fingers of your left hand that have let go.

The most important point about grip pressure is that it should remain constant throughout the swing. A sudden change in grip pressure at any time during the swing can change the path of the club or after the angle of the clubface, resulting in a missed shot. Consistent grip pressure goes a long way toward making you a more consistent golfer, in terms of ball contact and accuracy.

The accompanying table summarizes the essential checkpoints of what I call the *neutral grip*.

CHECKPOINTS OF THE NEUTRAL GRIP

LEFT HAND

1) The handle of the club lies between the first and second finger joints and rests at the base of the other two fingers.

2) Your thumb rides down the top of the handle slightly to the right of center and sits at 1:00. Your thumb is neither stretched down too far nor held up too short.

3) The heel pad of your palm rides on top of the handle.

4) The last two fingers of your left hand exert a bit more pressure than the other fingers.

RIGHT HAND

1) The little finger of your right hand either interlocks with the index finger of your left hand, or sits on top of the crevice formed by the index and middle fingers of your left hand.

2) The club is gripped more by the fingers than by the palm.

3) The thumb pad of your right hand completely covers your left thumb.

4) The index finger is separated from the other fingers of your right hand and forms a kind of hook.

5) The thumb of your right hand angles from right to left across the top of the handle, and sits at 11:00.

HANDS TOGETHER

1) The V's formed by the thumb and index finger of both hands point toward your right shoulder.

2) The palms of your hands face each other, or the back of your left hand faces directly at the target, and the back of your right hand faces directly away from the target.

It takes time to perfect a good grip and make it feel natural. The best way for a beginner to do that is to hold a club at times away from the golf course. Do this as often as practical. Once you have learned to grip a club correctly, it is like riding a bicycle. You never really forget how and can reclaim the skill quickly even if it vanishes from time to time.

Changing Grip — What I have described so far is the neutral grip. It's the best starting point for all occasional golfers. But because individual swings are different, it may be necessary for you to make small changes in the basic checkpoints. When you have a good understanding of the neutral grip, you may consider the following changes:

If you have a tendency to hit your shots to the right of your target, by either pushing or slicing the ball, you might have to align both hands a little more *to the right on the club handle*. This points the V's to the outside of the right shoulder, promoting an easier turning of the hands in the downswing. It also places the clubface squarely to the target at impact.

If you intentionally want to hook a ball — hit it from right to left to get around an obstacle — rotate both hands even more to the right.

If your normal shots tend to go to the left of your target — either straight to the left, or with a hook — you might have to align both hands a little more *to the left* on the club handle. This points the V's to the inside of your right shoulder. If you intentionally want to *slice* or *fade* a ball (hit it from left to right) — to get around an obstacle — then rotate both hands even more to the left.

I don't recommend extreme grip changes. That can restrict your natural swinging motion. But small changes can help. If you get confused, or if the changes don't do what you expect, always go back to the neutral grip.

THE ADDRESS

The address position involves some of the most important fundamentals in golf. Although we refer to the address as a "position," it's really a combination of subordinate positions. The placement of your feet on the parallel line, for example, and the distribution of your body weight, the alignment of the ball—even how you hold your chin—are all part of the address position. To play target golf well you must learn to address the ball consistently. To do this you need to build sound habits from the beginning.

Two basic reference points will help your position at address:

Imagine two lines forming the frame of a "railroad track" stretching out to the target area. One is the *target line,* which runs through the center of the ball to the target itself. The other line runs parallel to the target line, and is called the *parallel line*. The clubhead rests on the target line. Your toes just touch the parallel line.

It is important to understand that your toes, and therefore your body, are along the parallel line, *not* the target line. Also, you should not adjust your body so it is aimed directly at the target. Your body aims to the left of the target; the club aims at the target. I will discuss this in more detail soon, under the heading *Standing "Square."*

TARGET LINE

PARALLEL
LINE

To develop a consistent address, your body and feet are on the parallel line. The clubhead swings down the target line to hit the ball.

Getting Up to the Ball—When you approach the ball to make your next shot, use a standard procedure from start to finish. This is what I mean by "getting up to the ball." The procedure for getting into the address position beside the ball should always begin from a few yards behind the ball as you face the target. This way you get a good overall view of your target and everything around it. From this perspective you can decide just what sort of shot you need, or want to play. You can better see the right route, and all of the wrong ones. It is the place from where you plan and visualize your shot.

Move up to the ball in a fairly wide semicircle, stepping up to it from an angle 90° to the target line. This final approach to the ball is better than from the oblique angle many players use because it promotes better visualization of your target. In other words, you get to see the target relative to the surrounding landscape. The more reference points you have, the better you will be able to address yourself square to the target.

Now, with only your left hand on the club, step in toward the ball with your right foot. Place the toes of your right foot on the parallel line at a 90° angle to the line. To begin with, the inside of your foot should be on a line about six inches behind the ball.

It is much easier to set up correctly when you start from an open position.

Your right foot should be perpendicular (90°) to the target line. Your left foot is opened about 20° off perpendicular.

At the same time you place your right foot, set the clubhead behind the ball with the club face at a 90° angle to the target line. Now place your right hand on the club and complete your grip.

Squaring the Clubface—The best guide for making sure that the clubface is square to the target is to check the first groove up from the bottom of the clubface. The target line should be perpendicular to this line. Many golfers make the mistake of using the very bottom edge of the club to set alignment. But the bottom, or *lead*, edge is not always designed to be straight, so it can be misleading.

With your right foot and clubhead in position, move the toes of your left foot forward onto the parallel line and about two or three inches ahead of the ball. This distance can vary a bit, depending on your personal ball-to-foot relationship, which I will discuss soon. Now angle your left foot off of the perpendicular and toward the target about 20°.

When you look down at your feet, the right one will be straight; the left one should be angled a bit to the left. This is the basic address position.

Standing "Square"—Your knees, hips, and shoulders must be "square" at address. To

TARGET LINE

In a "square" stance, lines connecting shoulders, hips and knees are practically parallel to the target line. Also, your feet are about shoulder-width apart.

help you understand this, imagine three horizontal lines—one of them connecting your knees, another your hips, a third your shoulders—all of them parallel to the target line. Your right shoulder will be a little lower than your left because your right hand is lower on the club, but the key thing is that all of the lines will be practically parallel to the target line. The result is that your body will be "square" at address.

Stance Width—The distance your feet are separated at address is measured from the *insides* of your feet. As a general rule, for full-swing shots the separation of your feet should be equal to the width of your shoulders. Obviously, there can be no standard separation for all golfers; everyone is built a little differently.

If you spread your feet too wide, however, you restrict body movement and lose flexibility and freedom to swing. The problem with a stance that is too narrow, on the other hand, is that you lose the ability to restrict motion in your lower body.

A few great players have successfully used a very narrow stance. The late Jimmy Demaret was one, but he had an exceptionally natural rhythm and ability to use his hands in the swing. Great golfers are often exceptions to rules that most golfers should follow.

The key to a correct stance width is balance. Set your feet wide enough apart to be able to maintain your balance *throughout* the swing. Your physical size will certainly be a factor in this, as will the tempo of your swing. If you are a tall person or have a fairly fast swing tempo, you will probably need a wider stance than if you are short or have a relatively slow swing tempo.

Start with the insides of your feet at shoulder width and adjust from there for balance and flexibility.

Distribution of Weight and Knee Flex—Bend your knees slightly at the address to help avoid body rigidity. Any stiffness prevents a fluid swing. Flex both knees to a one-quarter sitting position, as shown in accompanying photos.

Your knees should also tilt inward toward each other, in a knock-kneed way. You should feel a slight pressure on the insides of your feet. This allows you to maintain your balance during the swing.

Overall body weight is distributed evenly, no more on one foot than on the other, and no more on your toes than on the heels. I like to feel that if someone gave me a shove in any direction when I'm at address, I would not easily lose my balance.

For the various specialty shots your weight may have to be distributed differently. I cover those variations in a separate chapter.

Distance from the Ball—There is no standard distance between you and the ball. Again, everyone is built differently. The distance is determined individually by the length of your arms. There is, however, a general rule to follow:

Leaning slightly forward, let your arms fall from the shoulders so your arms hand straight down. This sets you at the correct distance from the ball. You won't be reaching out too far with your arms held rigid, nor pulling in too close with your arms bent at the elbows and too close to your body. You want to be in the most natural body position you can achieve in all aspects of the address.

Of course, the length of the club you use will also determine how far you actually stand from the ball. You will be slightly farther away with a driver, the longest club, than with the pitching wedge, the shortest club. But regardless of the club in use, the best check of your distance from the ball is to lean forward at the waist and let your arms hang straight down.

Ball-to-Foot Relationship—The last fundamental in the address position is the alignment of the ball relative to your feet. You must pay particular attention to the left foot.

For iron shots, you want to strike the ball with a slightly descending blow—the clubhead moving downward at impact. Therefore, the ball should be placed just behind the lowest point in your swing. For most golfers, this means that the ball is lined up about two inches inside the left heel.

In my opinion, it is best that all iron shots—from the #2 iron down to the wedge—be played from the same position, about two inches inside your left heel. I recommend the same alignment for fairway woods—the #3, #4, and #5 woods—when they are played off the ground.

There is little difference between the setup for the wedge and driver. Club length and lie change, not the stance.

Arms should fall from your shoulders in a natural position.

The clubhead should be moving downward at impact, striking the ball just below its center.

For all shots played off the ground, the ball should be two to three inches inside your left heel.

When hitting the ball off the tee with the driver, you should line up the ball off the instep or heel of your left foot. This will put it just forward of the lowest point in the swing. The clubhead should be just beginning its upward arc when it hits the ball. This sweeps the the ball off the tee. If you drive the ball off the tee with an iron, do not place the ball differently than for any other iron shot. The ball is placed forward for the driver because the driver doesn't supply sufficient loft.

When setting up for a tee shot, line up the ball with the instep or heel of your left foot.

Finding Your Low Point—Every golfer can find his or her individual low point in the swing. It takes only a couple of practice swings. Take your address position and make a practice swing that is an exact simulation of how you actually swing at the ball. Notice where the club first hits, or grazes, the top of the ground. That is your low point. Now, "mark" the low point relative to the proper positioning of your feet and determine where you must align the ball at the address.

Posture—Your overall posture at address is essential to making your best swing. Though there is a slight flex in your knees, your back is straight as you bend slightly forward at the waist. Do not slump your shoulders forward. Bend only at the waist. Feel tall at the ball!

Proper posture is balanced and relaxed.

SUMMARY

The accompanying box summarizes checkpoints for a good address. Use it to develop good habits.

All of the details of the grip and address may seem like a great many things to remember and execute—and they are! But after applying these principles in your play, doing them automatically will become easy. They will be part of a fluid approach and stroke.

CHECKPOINTS OF A SOUND ADDRESS

1) Place the toes of your right foot on the parallel line. Make sure that your right foot is at a 90° angle to the parallel and to begin with about six inches behind the ball.

2) Place your left foot on the parallel line at an angle about 20° off of perpendicular.

3) Align the ball approximately two inches inside your left heel for iron shots and for fairway woods played off the ground. Align the ball with your left heel or instep when you are using the driver off the tee.

4) Spread your feet approximately shoulder-width apart.

5) Imagine three parallel horizontal lines connecting your knees, hips, and shoulders. Make sure these lines are parallel to the parallel line and you will be standing square at address.

6) Lean forward slightly and let your arms hang naturally from your shoulders. This determines the distance you should be from the ball at address.

7) Distribute your body weight evenly on the center of both feet.

8) Flex your knees slightly.

9) Keep your back straight and bend slightly at the waist. Don't tuck your chin into your chest.

GOLF TIP

Pro shops are selling more and more lightweight golfshoes. These give support, and some are even spikeless shoes. Some courses don't allow spikeless shoes, although USGA tests show they do no more damage to greens than spiked shoes.

CHAPTER TWO

The Backswing

The motion of the backswing involves three distinct muscle groups: the muscles of the lower body—your feet, legs and hips—which provide the foundation and balance point for all golf swings; the muscles of your arms, shoulders and upper back, which provide the coiling power required in the backswing; and the more delicate muscles of your hands and wrists, which hinge, or cock, to set the clubhead into position at the top of the stroke. In this chapter we will analyze the backswing in detail and show how all those different muscle groups come into play.

At all times you should be aware that you have aligned with a specific target and that the moves of the backswing are in conjunction with this target.

BACKSWING MECHANICS

A truism about the backswing is that the best players of the game develop the ability to keep the clubhead square throughout the swing. That is, the angle of the clubface does not change from its position at address. In my experience, novice golfers lose the angle of the clubface as early as six inches into the backswing. They seldom correct it by impact because they try to manipulate the club with their hands. And that is the chief reason why they are not consistently accurate with their shots.

Luckily, this is a problem you can overcome. By applying simple principles of the target game you can develop an effective backswing.

Initial Motion—The start of the backswing is a unified motion of arms and shoulders. Your hands follow along freely but are basically passive at this point—they do not hinge. Your elbows should remain pointed toward your hips, and your arms should not stretch away from or across your body. Most of the coiling effort should be felt with the back of your left shoulder blade.

At this early stage your legs should be "alert" and flexible. Your right knee is braced and slightly flexed to the left.

At this point in the backswing, your hands are not moving independently; they are simply following along with the coiling of your upper body. As a result the clubface is beginning to open slightly relative to the target, but it has not yet moved out of a horizontal plane.

And, although you have not tried in any way to control the path of the clubhead, it will, as your body coils, begin to move gradually inside the target line.

Midway through the backswing, the toe of the clubhead points straight up.

When the backswing is half finished, the club should be parallel to the ground and the target line, with the toe of the clubhead pointing to the sky. Your upper-body coil is almost complete, and the strenuous part of the backswing is done.

Halfway Checkpoint—If the club is not parallel to the ground, or the toe of the club is not pointing straight up, you have probably hinged or cocked your wrists too soon. To break this habit, practice swinging the club back by just coiling your upper body.

Another reason why the club may be out of position is that you are moving your legs too much, which causes imbalance. Your right knee should be flexed in toward your left leg, and most of your weight should be on your right foot.

Taking the Club Up—With your upper-body coiling just about completed, you have moved the club in a low sweep away from the ball and must now start to move it more vertically. At this point your wrists begin to hinge, or cock. If your hands and wrists are tense at this stage, hinging will not occur properly, and your arms will stretch and lift the

Also midway through the backswing, the club shaft is parallel to the target line.

club in an attempt to complete the backswing. Stretching and lifting in this way will cause the club to swing out of its natural plane.

You should feel your arms slowing down, allowing your hands to "set" the club over your right shoulder. The hinging and setting actions also pull your left shoulder back behind the ball a little bit more. Because you have already moved your left shoulder behind the ball with your coiling motion, the final setting of the club should not be done too strenuously.

DON'T DO THIS!
Here, I swung the club back without coiling my shoulders. Notice that my hips and legs slide. They don't coil as they should.

CHECKPOINTS FOR COMPLETED BACKSWING

1) The shaft of the club is "set" over your right shoulder parallel to the ground with the longest clubs, a bit short of parallel with shorter clubs. The toe of the club is pointed toward the ground, and the shaft should also be parallel to the target line.

2) Your left wrist is straight, neither flexed nor hyperextended.

3) Your thumbs are on a line between your arms. Your left thumb is under the handle of the club supporting it.

What Your Legs Do—I don't want to give you the impression that the backswing is the product of your arms, shoulders and hands only. Your legs have some work to do too. Otherwise, the backswing will not be as full or as fluid as it should be.

Basically your legs maintain balance. They keep your body stable, letting it flow into a full and free swing.

As your upper body coils, your weight transfers to your right leg. It is very important at this point that your weight shifts to the inside of your right foot. Promote this by standing with your right knee slightly knock-kneed at address. When this is done correctly, you'll feel a little resistance in your knee and pressure along the inside of your right foot.

The result of this weight shift is a sort of springboard effect for the start of the downswing. I like to think of the right leg as being in a bracing position, so that at any time in the backswing it is ready to start the downswing, to move forward toward the target.

Mechanics of Weight Transfer—It is very important that your body weight is *not* transferred to the *outside* of your right foot. That leads to what is called *sway,* in which the body moves sideways rather than coiling. If you sway in the backswing, one of two things will happen in the downswing, both of them producing an ineffective stroke. For one, you will probably sway in the downswing too—moving the body laterally past the ball before it is struck. This brings the clubhead to impact at an angle that pops the ball weakly into the air or drives it down into the ground.

If you sway on the backswing, and coil your body to the left on the downswing, you will pull the club across the ball from outside to inside the target line. The ball will either be pulled badly to the left, or sliced to the right of the target.

You can avoid these problems by transferring weight to the inside of your right foot, as described and illustrated.

DON'T DO THIS!
If your right knee buckles, coiling is inhibited. Sway will occur.

Your right leg remains slightly flexed in the backswing as it takes on the job of carrying body weight. As your body coils away from the target, your left knee must help by folding in toward your right knee. This permits a smooth transfer of weight to your right side, and a complete coil. The braced right knee with your weight on the inside of your right foot moderates the motion.

Your left knee can fold in a certain kind of way, however, and still restrict the coiling of the body. That's when your knee is pointing toward the ball. If your left knee gets into this position, it is a sign that you haven't transferred your weight to your right foot, and your body coil may be restricted. The left side of the body will be tilted downward at the completion of the backswing instead of coiled naturally to a position just behind the ball.

DON'T DO THIS!
Another common error is lifting the club to complete the backswing rather than letting the wrists hinge and set the club. Notice how the whole body is out of position here.

Remember, consciously fold your left knee back toward your right knee. At the end of the backswing, there should be only a slight bit of weight on your left side. Most of the weight is on your right leg.

Lifting your left heel assists proper movement of the left leg. How much the heel rises depends on your flexibility. A very supple person won't need much lift to create a nice flow and a full body motion. People with tighter muscles may need more rise out of the left foot. Your body will tell you how much you need but, one way or the other, let it happen. Trying to keep your heel on the ground creates unnecessary and possibly troublesome body tension.

A Word on Head Movement—Another tenet of golf instruction over the years has been the admonition to "Keep the head still" during the swing. I don't advocate that, but I don't suggest a lot of movement either. High-speed photography has shown that even the most expert golfers will move their heads a little.

By trying to keep your head perfectly still you create tension that prevents a full coiling of your shoulders and proper weight transfer to your right side. Instead, try to keep your neck muscles relaxed. In the backswing it is OK if your head moves slightly to the right as long as your legs maintain balance.

My instruction is to always keep your eyes trained on the back of the ball throughout the swing because that's where you want the clubhead to make contact. Concentration there promotes hand-to-eye coordination, which is important in making solid contact. It also helps to control your head movement so it is neither too much nor too little, and helps keep you aware of where the clubhead should strike the ball.

PRE-BACKSWING PREPARATION

Many people assume that golf is easy because the ball is not moving before it is hit. They add that the golfer is not forced to swing the club at a given moment—he has all the time he needs to set up before making the stroke.

This is the correct position: Hands between the elbows and the shaft on a line parallel to the target line.

At the top of the backswing: Notice that the thumb of my left hand is under the club handle. Also, my shoulders are coiled behind the ball. The downswing is about to begin.

Actually, the static aspect of golf makes the game *difficult* to play well. Odd as it may seem, having to initiate *all* of the movement in the game can strain mental and physical concentration, especially when there *is* so much time between shots. On average, you hit a golf shot every four or five minutes during a round. Having to start the body in motion from a static position is always more awkward than if you're already on the go.

For these reasons, you will see the best golfers creating a certain amount of body and club movement *while at address* without changing their carefully prepared positions. You will note too, that they do not take a great deal of time to play shots. This part of my backswing instruction deals with developing that approach. You want to "turn on the ignition" to get your golf machine running. Even though this is not part of the swing itself, it is essential to making a fluid and effective stroke toward the target.

Rock the Boat—When you get into your final address position—feet in place and properly aligned relative to the ball, your body aimed correctly and in good posture—rock back and forth on your feet a few times. Wiggle your toes and heels, and raise and lower them a few times. *Do this without altering your basic foot positions.*

This will give your body motion and help you adjust the distribution of your weight. You will find a *balance point* that gives you a good foundation on which to perform the backswing.

Squeeze and Release the Grip—At the same time you are rocking on your feet, try squeezing and releasing the grip. Here again, you do the movement without changing the address. The position of your hands remains as you fixed it when you set up at the address.

Loosen your fingers on the shaft, then press them back onto the handle. Do this a few times. This is a particularly good pre-backswing movement because it helps you find just the right grip pressure.

Golfers tend to grip the club too tightly from anxiety over the last or next shot. When your hands are too tight, tension works up into arms and shoulders. Without relief from this tension before the backswing begins, the initial parts of the backswing will be jerky, uneven, and too fast. The rest of the swing probably won't be very good, either.

Waggle with Purpose—Probably the most common movement before the backswing is the *waggle*. Waggling is an instinctive thing. All golfers do it, even those with a club in their hands for the very first time. To waggle, swing the club a few feet back and forth behind the ball, or behind and forward of it, or up and down. This gets your hands and arms in motion, frees them of tension, and gives them feeling and flexibility. You can even go so far as to cock and release your wrists during the waggle.

The waggle is a good pre-backswing action regardless of how you do it. As I mentioned, many golfers waggle the club by raising it up and down. Others swing the club back and forth *above* the ball. Neither of those actions represents what will actually happen in your swing. You have no intention of swinging the club *above* the ball and, I hope, you are not going to swing it straight up and down, either. Why then inject a movement into your "muscle memory" that you don't want and can't use?

That's why I've developed a waggle that is a kind of sneak preview of the full swing. I waggle by swinging the club back and forth *behind* the ball and *on the same level with it*. It is not unlike what a pool player does with his cuestick, sliding it back and forth just behind the cueball before hitting it.

You can do even more with your waggle in the way of a rehearsal of your swing. You can simulate the *tempo* of the swing you will make. Waggle the club at the same pace you intend to use for your shot. This will vary. When you're hitting a driver off the tee on a long hole, you are going to make a fairly aggressive swing. Waggle accordingly, with a bit of an upbeat. When you're hitting a short chip shot from the fringe of a green, for which you need a gentler touch, waggle the club softly and slowly.

Finally, and perhaps most important, the waggle gives you a chance to relate the actual swing to the intended target.

As you "read" these photos from right to left, notice that in the second photo the hands have moved slightly forward to start the flow of motion in the swing.

Because the waggle is intended to give you a feel of both the clubhead and the path of the backswing, you will use more hand action than in the initial stages of the backswing itself. The waggle I recommend gives you an opportunity to simulate parts of your swing before actually hitting the ball.

The Forward Press—Although the preliminary movements made with your feet, hands and waggle have given you a certain momentum, there is nonetheless, a moment of stillness before you begin the backswing. It starts when you set the club behind the ball and hold it in place. It is only the briefest of pauses, but it does interrupt the flow of motion you've generated. You can bring that flow back with what I call the *forward press*.

The forward press is a movement with your hands very slightly to the left, toward the target. It is not a big move—as shown above. This tiny movement is actually the first part of the backswing. You make the forward press, then move the club directly into the backswing.

The forward press is to golf what the slight lean forward is to the baseball pitcher beginning his windup. It starts the flow of motion. Indeed, it makes the motion flow.

Concentration—Does reading this advice make it seem that there is too much to do and think about? Don't worry. Once you get into the habit of doing these various actions, they will meld into one. All together, they take less than 30 seconds, but to do them well, you have to concentrate.

It has been shown, scientifically, that watching a moving object keeps us more alert than when we are looking at a stationary object. In addition, it is quite possible to stare at the golf ball for too long. You may even "forget" what you are there to do, and lose concentration.

CHECKPOINTS OF A PROPER BACKSWING

1) Waggle with a purpose. Use the waggle to practice tempo and to practice a level backswing directly away from your intended target.

2) Use a slight forward press to get the backswing started fluidly.

3) Your legs should be "alert" and flexible. Brace your right knee and slightly flex it to the left.

4) Start the clubhead moving directly away from the target by coiling your upper body.

5) When the club is first parallel to the ground, the toe should be pointing to the sky and the shaft should be on a line direct to the target.

6) To complete the backswing, your arms should slow down. Your wrists should hinge to set the club over your shoulder.

7) At the top of the backswing, the shaft of the club should again be on a direct line to the target.

8) Also at the top of the backswing your shoulders should be coiled behind the ball and your weight should be on the inside of your right foot.

That's why golf should be played quickly. I strongly urge a quicker pace, especially when in the address position. It will also help you to keep your concentration.

As you move from shot to shot, think about what you want to do. Consider the alternatives, try to gauge the wind, choose the best route to the green, and so on. When you get to your ball, calculate your yardage and what club you will need to get your ball to your chosen target. Fix the target in your mind's eye, then play the shot. Slow golf will hurt your chances of doing well. It will make you freeze up from tension or simply make you stop concentrating.

GOLF TIP

When driving, an experienced player may want to tee the ball a little higher and more forward in the stance. This allows him to strike the ball as the clubhead is slightly in the upswing. The result is more carry of the ball through the air and thus a longer drive, especially in wet conditions.

CHAPTER THREE

The Downswing

The downswing is essentially a reversal of the backswing. It begins at the peak of the backswing, travels through the same lane established by the backswing, and continues until the clubhead strikes the ball. The challenge of this stroke is to make the transition from backswing to downswing through the plane established by the backswing with little or no alteration. The overall goal is to return the clubhead through the ball to the target. The mechanics I discuss are merely a means of achieving this goal. Each particular move makes it easier to swing through the ball to the target.

STOP, PROCEED OR PAUSE?

You can't stop at the top of the backswing, if only because the essential purpose of the backswing is to develop momentum and sufficient force. Stopping the club, a difficult thing to do in any case, would defeat that purpose. Neither can you simply keep the club going. That would be tough to do without rushing the swing and destroying your overall timing. There is a middle choice.

Start Down with the Left Foot—My approach to reversing the direction of the club is a sort of pause: Just as the club is nearing the completion of the backswing, your raised left heel drops back to the ground as though feeling for secure footing. This creates the "pause" between backswing and downswing. I prefer to think of it however, as a blend of motions—your upper body almost stopping its turning action as your weight settles back onto your left foot.

This is a subtle move, but dropping the left heel back to the ground creates just enough of a pause to give you a smooth transition, one that is neither rushed nor hesitant.

Reversing Continued—Think of the dropping of your left heel to the ground as transitional. It's a movement that trips the switch to project a backward film of your backswing. Every detail of every movement of your backswing is repeated, exactly. Only this time in reverse. This time you are watching your downswing.

Some golfers tend to use their shoulders to start the downswing. As a result they slice the ball, or pull it badly to the left of the target. When your shoulders move first, your arms and club come out of the plane established by the backswing. The club is pulled across the ball from outside to inside the target line. In the backswing the club was swung inside that line; it should also swing back to the ball inside the target line.

DON'T DO THIS!
Here's the result of using your shoulders to bring the club down and through. Your body is pulled and spun away from the target line.

DON'T DO THIS!
The result of an early spin-out in the downswing is a weight reversal that will cause many problems.

As you moved the club away from the ball in the backswing, you made a full coil of your shoulders very early in the action, with little or no hand motion. The clubhead traveled in a flat arc fairly close to the ground for the first half of the backswing.

In the second half of the backswing, your shoulders turned very little and your hands hinged to produce a nearly vertical positioning of the clubhead. The last move in the backswing was with your hands—the hinging that set the club over your right shoulder.

Now, if the downswing is to be an exact reversal of the backswing, your hands should begin the downward swing of the club. Their major contribution in the backswing was to produce the vertical positioning of the clubhead. Their major contribution in the downswing is to start the club moving toward the ball in that same plane. When the clubhead is moving downward, your upper body can start to turn. As you start the downswing, there is a tendency to hit at the ball. But you want it to be smooth, without forced acceleration.

What you want to do is "hit in-place" during the first part of the downswing—that is, keep your shoulders coiled and square and *pull the club straight down* with your hands. As the clubhead gets moving, your body starts to spring into action.

Pulling the Club Straight Down—Your hands should begin to release, or uncock, at the start of the downswing. If done correctly, the release *can't* start too soon. The key to the action is the direction your hands take as they begin to uncock. As I mentioned, that direction is straight down.

That "straight down" action is the first move in the downswing, after the left heel drops to create the transition from backswing to downswing. You pull the club through as though it were the cord on a window shade. At the same time, your hands begin to uncock. But because your hands are moving vertically, they can't be "thrown" or "cast" out away from you. They will start to uncock, and they should be allowed to, but the clubhead still remains inside the target line until it reaches the ball.

By "hitting in place," you let the club return directly back to the ball. Your left shoulder is on the parallel line.

This is a front view of the shot shown on page 45. Notice that the left foot is firmly planted. The right knee is pressing to the left and the left shoulder is on the parallel line.

Move to the Left—Even though I talk about individual movements in the swing, each actually works in close coordination with other moves. For example, when your hands pull the club down vertically to start the downswing, your raised left heel will already have lowered so it is flat on the ground. You should feel your entire left side becoming firm, which is good because you want to feel very solidly planted on your left side. The downward thrust of your hands and club reinforces this sense.

Your *left leg should not stiffen*. It should be slightly flexed. For the longer shots you play, when your swing is naturally a little harder, there will even be a slightly outward bow in your left leg as the club hits the ball.

If your left leg stiffens in the downswing, you have not shifted your weight sufficiently to that side, and you will probably fall back—a move you definitely want to avoid.

At the beginning of the downswing, then, there is a movement to the left, a movement that combines a weight shift and a rotation of your left hip. For as soon as your weight is shifted to your left leg, your left hip will begin to rotate upon the firm foundation established by the weight shift. Think of your left hip as a hinge and your right side the door that turns upon the hinge.

The gradual release or uncocking of your hands at the start of the downswing is important to this returning to the left side. The reason many golfers continue moving laterally in the downswing and get their hips ahead of the ball at impact is that their hands are locked. Because his hands are not active, the golfer instinctively keeps moving his body laterally to bring the clubhead to the ball. The instinct is correct, but in this case misused.

When you release your hands at the beginning of the downswing, the clubhead is set in motion toward the ball and your body naturally beings to turn to stay in balance. The unhinging of your hands is what starts the lateral shift of weight to your left.

Here, my hands have unhinged, my left knee is slightly bowed and my right side is moving through to the left.

HAND ACTION

The proper release of your hands in the downswing is a natural action done in conjunction with your forearm. In other words, both forearms and wrists rotate back to the left as the clubhead releases. You have to let it happen. It starts at the beginning of the downswing, and at the bottom of the downswing, it creates a real "hitting" motion. Here's the image I want you to have: When the release of your hands is complete — at impact — you are hitting the ball with the *back* of your left hand. The clubface and the back of your left hand are square to the target.

It is this movement of your hands that fires the clubhead at the target. It is a movement very much like throwing a Frisbee left-handed. At the very bottom of the downswing you fling your left hand — your left elbow pulls in toward your body and the back of your left hand turns to face away from the ball after impact.

You can practice this feeling. A drill is described in chapter 9. There you'll find other useful tips and drills for better target golf.

In this swing, the back of the left hand is square to the target line at impact.

The release of the left hand in a proper golf swing feels like a left-handed Frisbee toss.

KNEE ACTION

The movement to the left is completed when your right knee "folds" and drives toward your left leg. Moving your right knee this way is not automatic. Once the hands reach waist height in the downswing, both the hands and right knee move together through impact.

If you move your right knee too soon, you will throw your right shoulder outward toward the ball and create an outside-to-inside swinging plane. If your knee does not kick in, or drive to the left, you will not complete the weight shift. Without completing the weight shift, you will have a difficult time properly releasing the clubhead. Most likely you will swing up too soon or hit behind the ball.

The right knee "folds" *laterally* to the left—it does not jut forward toward the ball—so that at the completion of the swing there is almost no gap between the two legs, and the right heel is well up off the ground.

At this point of the downswing, your right knee has moved up to the left and your right heel is off the ground.

These are back and side views of the same phase of the downswing — the end of the shot. At this stage, your body should be balanced on the left side and facing the target. Practically all of your weight is off the right foot and on the ouside of the left foot.

CHECKPOINTS OF A PROPER DOWNSWING

KEY MOVEMENTS

1) Plant your left heel firmly on the ground. Keep your left knee slightly flexed and bowed outward. These movements will firm up your left side, and enable you to swing the clubhead through the ball and to the target.

2) Pull your hands straight down, almost vertically, to release them from the hinged or cocked position. Think "immediate release" or you will not release your hands in time to make proper contact with the ball.

3) Swing smoothly *without forced acceleration.*

4) Drive your right knee toward your left leg, almost closing the gap between your legs.

5) Shift your weight to the left as your clubhead begins to move toward the ball.

6) Imagine that your solidly set up left side is the hinge upon which the "door" of your right side turns.

7) Move fluidly but at maximum speed through impact and into your follow-through. Your position at follow-through is a direct reflection of the moves you made during the downswing, and will have you facing the target.

FOLLOW-THROUGH POSITIONS

1) You are standing erect with good balance. Your shoulders are up; your right foot is up on its toes; and your weight is on the outside of your left foot.

2) Your left knee is bowed and in front of your left foot. If you regularly make a proper weight shift you will wear down the left side of your left shoe.

3) The front of your body is facing the target. Your hands are over your left shoulder. Your thumbs are under the handle of the club. The right hand is behind the left, indicating that you have made a full release of your hands.

CHAPTER FOUR

The Swing At Work

My experience has shown me that beginners and intermediate golfers usually develop a better understanding of the mechanics of the overall swing when they have studied the backswing and downswing separately. For that reason I have given you a detailed, step-by-step explanation of the backswing and the downswing.

It is also important, however, to understand the backswing and downswing as they are integrated into the whole golf swing. For that reason I bring them together in this chapter. In subsequent chapters I will give you advice on how to target every golf shot, from the drive to the putt.

Let's go to the first tee and imagine we are about to tee off. My intent is to give a step-by-step procedure in how to take your game from the practice tee to the golf course.

PRE-SWING ACTIONS

1) If you are using your driver off the tee, tee the ball up so only half of it is above the clubface when the clubface is set behind the ball at address. Tee the ball lower for tee shots played with fairway woods and irons.

2) After you have teed the ball up, step back a few yards directly behind the ball and face the target. This gives you an overall view of your situation. It is the best place from which to pick out your target line and create a mental image of the kind of shot you want to play.

For most shots off the tee, set up the ball with your fingers between the ball and the ground.

3) After deciding on the type of shot you want to play, and the direction you want it to take, think of one checkpoint in the swing that you think will help you hit the ball well. This can be any mechanical point you have been working on. For example, it may be the position of your left hand on the grip, the turn of your left shoulder away from the ball, or the slowing of your arms during the downswing.

For a driver shot, half of the ball should be above the clubface. Tee the ball lower for shots played with irons and fairway woods.

This kind of concentration not only helps reduce any tension or anxiety you might have about the shot, it also stimulates a good swing. But, you should pick only one checkpoint to work on this way. No one can play a good golf shot with his mind overloaded with technical points.

4) When you move into the address position and set-up beside the ball, check to see that your grip is correct and your grip pressure is the way you like it. Check the ball alignment relative to the positioning of your feet. Look at the target and trace a line from it back to your ball. That establishes the expected flight path of the ball to the target. Then take your waggles and swing. Very little time should elapse between your look at the target, your waggle, and your swing.

FIRST HALF OF THE SWING

1) Waggle the club a few times. Tighten and loosen your grip. Then make a slight forward press of the hands. This forward press should lead directly into a coiling or turning of your left shoulder and arm to the right. Your right leg braces. The club swings to the inside of the target line.

2) Your left knee bends toward the right knee to allow a full coil of the body and a complete weight shift to the inside of the right foot.

3) When the club is parallel to the ground and its toe is pointing up, your hands begin to hinge, or cock. This hinging helps bring the club up over your right shoulder, and you do not need to stretch or lift your arms to complete the backswing.

4) At the top of the backswing, the wrist hinging is completed so that both thumbs are directly under the clubhandle. The toe of the club is pointing toward the ground. Most of your weight is on the inside of your right foot. Your left heel is raised off the ground. Your eyes are on the back of the ball.

SECOND HALF OF THE SWING

1) To start the downswing, drop your raised left heel to the ground and pull the club straight down with your hands. At the same time, begin unhinging your hands. This is called the *release*. The release should become a natural action. Do not restrict that unhinging.

2) Your weight has shifted to your left side, which makes that side firm. Your left leg is very slightly flexed and bowed outward. Your hips begin to turn or rotate counterclockwise.

3) Your right knee drives toward the left leg, almost closing the gap between your legs.

4) Your arms and body move as a single unit—there is no separation. You feel that your arms are slowing down, or at least slowing down relative to the clubhead.

GOLF TIP

If warm-up time is limited, practice swinging by using two clubs. Be sure to let shoulders turn and back muscles loosen.

IMPACT AND FOLLOW-THROUGH

1) At impact, your hands have fully unhinged. The back of your left hand and the clubface are "square" to the target line.

2) After impact, your hands continue turning over so your thumbs are facing the sky. The action is as though you were flinging a Frisbee with your left hand.

3) At follow-through you should be standing erect, balanced and facing the target.

4) Your shoulders are up. Your right foot is on its toes. Your weight is on the outside of your left foot. A golfer who regularly makes a proper weight shift will wear down the left side of his left shoe.

5) Your left leg is now straight.

6) Your hands are over your left shoulder. Your thumbs are under the handle of the club, indicating a full release of your hands at impact.

These are the essential elements of *every* non-putting golf shot. It's OK to vary from the procedures given here. The important thing is that you have a routine, a set procedure that you repeat every time. This is the best way to develop consistent, relaxed shotmaking. When you are shooting in a familiar pattern, you will be more comfortable and less anxious about your performance.

As I have noted earlier, all of the mechanical details described and illustrated here may at first seem like too much to think about. But the more you play and the more you practice with these principles in mind, the sooner they will become part of your game—good habits that result in lower scores. They will meld into a single, unified action.

THE PROPER SWING

The following picture sequences are two views of essentially the same shot—a complete and correct golf swing. "Read" them from left to right to page 59. Review the sequences a few times and reread this chapter until you are sure that you can replay the picture series mentally on the course.

CHAPTER SIX

The Chipping Game

Greens have the shortest grass on the golf course, making them the smoothest and fastest-running surfaces. The area immediately surrounding them is called the *fringe* or *collar*. Fringe grass is sometimes only a little longer than the grass on the greens, and almost as smooth.

You can putt the ball if it is on the fringe no more than a foot off the green. When the ball is farther back on the fringe, however, it is not such a good idea to putt because you must roll the ball over two different lengths of grass. That makes it difficult to determine how hard to hit the ball. Furthermore, no matter how smooth the fringe grass may be, it can produce odd bounces. For these reasons, it is best to hit a *chip* shot.

The chip is a shot with just enough loft to get the ball over the fringe and onto the green. Direction and distance are the primary considerations of the chip shot. Getting the ball into the air is of minimal concern. In these respects the chip shot is closely related to putting. The ball is meant to roll most of the way. Even so, the chip must carry a short distance in the air, and therefore requires a technique of its own.

The chip shop is aptly named. It is a relatively short stroke. You don't take the club back very far, and there is not much follow-through. It is basically a simple shot, not a problem or hazard shot. A well-executed chip gets you down in two, meaning that you expect to get the ball close enough to the hole so you can easily putt the next shot into the cup.

CLUB SELECTION FOR CHIPPING

I see far too many golfers using the pitching wedge to play all of their chip shots. That may be because they use this club so much in other parts of their games. Out of habit, or familiarity, they chip with it even when it lessens their chances of getting the ball close to the hole.

I usually advise against the wedge for a chip shot because the wedge is the most lofted club in the bag. It is meant for hitting the ball high. And, as mentioned, height is not important to the chip shot. There are no hazards and rarely a high hill to get over. The higher a ball goes, the harder it is to hit it straight and the correct distance.

On the other hand, the lower you hit a golf ball the straighter you can hit it, and the better you can control distance. Essentially, the sooner you can get the ball rolling, the better off you are.

In spite of this advice, you *can* use the pitching wedge to chip, but only under special circumstances. I'll discuss those later on.

Use Irons—The chip is generally played with the #9, #8, #7, #6 and #5 irons, although some players can get the job done with less-lofted clubs.

On shots like this, use enough loft to carry the ball over the fringe and still let the ball roll as much as possible. To make this shot, I'm using a #7 iron.

The decision as to which club to use for chipping depends primarily on how much green is between the ball and hole. The average chip shot is between 25 and 50 feet long, total distance, and from 5 to 10 feet off the green.

Here's the basic rule: The closer your ball is to the green, the less-lofted club you need. For example, if you are three feet off the green for a shot of 40 feet or more, use the #5 iron. For each additional two feet of distance from the edge of the green, use the next higher club.

For chips shorter than 40 feet to the cup, no matter how far you are off the fringe, use the more-lofted clubs. The breakdown, in this case, is based on the amount of green you have on which to roll the ball. If you have 40 feet, use the #8 iron. If the distance is 30 feet, use the #9 iron. When the pin is closer than 30 feet, then you can use the pitching wedge.

Exceptions—This club-selection strategy is not absolute. You must be prepared to adapt to particular conditions. For example, if you have a 45-foot chip downhill on a fast-running green, use a more-lofted club—a #9 iron or pitching wedge—to keep the ball from going too far.

Conversely, if you are shooting uphill to a hole only 25 feet away, you may need a #7 iron to get the ball to run up the slope.

Also, if the ball is down low in some long, tangled fringe grass, you will probably have to use a lofted club no matter the length of the shot. Your main goal in this case is to get the ball cleanly on its way.

With experience you will come up with a club-selection system that suits your touch for these shots. Everyone's touch is a little different. Base your system on the following two guidelines:

1) Don't loft the ball any more than you have to.
2) Always land the ball on the green.

CHIPPING TECHNIQUE

Whatever your personal touch for the chip shot, it should be based on hitting the ball the same way every time. With this kind of consistency you can be a much better judge of distance and direction for any type of chip. To that end there is a near-universal method for hitting the shot.

Chip Grip—Use the same grip as you used for your regular shots. Grip pressure should be firm, but not tight, because you want to make a crisp stroke.

With this in mind, choke down on the handle at least a few inches to enhance club control and feel. Also, by choking down you can hit the chip with a little more acceleration of the clubhead.

Because the chip is a delicate, finesse shot, golfers worry about hitting the ball too far, especially when playing the less-lofted #5, #6 and #7 irons. They tend to slow the clubhead at impact. Choking down on the handle will reduce that tendency.

Chip Address—Use an open stance. Your left foot is pulled well back from the parallel line, and both feet are angled at least 30° to the left. You are almost directly facing the target. This allows the club to swing freely through impact, out toward the target.

Your feet are quite close together, perhaps only a couple of inches apart, and your weight is predominantly on your left foot—distributed about 75% to 25% in favor of the left side. Your weight should stay on your left side for the entire shot.

Your hands are slightly ahead of the ball at address to assure crisp ball contact. You definitely want to hit the ball first, before the clubhead strikes the ground.

Play the ball about two inches inside your left heel. Because your feet are so close together, and your hands are ahead of the ball, it may appear that the ball is aligned farther to the right in your stance. But you can easily check alignment by following your eye from the leading edge of the club back to your feet. With the ball two inches inside your left heel, it should be at the low point in your downswing.

Aim the clubhead directly at the target. Stance is open for a free swing.

HOW TO USE VIDEO TO IMPROVE YOUR GAME

Many of today's teaching pros use video as a teaching aid. I heartily endorse this. You may have a mental image of what his swing looks like, but more than likely it's quite different from the actual swing. It's sometimes quite difficult to correct a mistake in your swing unless you can actually watch that mistake in action.

Not all teaching professionals have video equipment, however, and not all people learning the game will be able to contract the services of a teaching pro. But you may have a friend tape your swing. If so, I offer the following tips:

CAMERA POSITION

The person holding the camera should be either directly to the side or directly behind the golfer. Any other angle will tend to distort vital aspects of the golf swing, such as correct setup, plane of swing, follow-through to target, etc.

I also suggest that each sequence be taped at least six successive times. You are unlikely to swing the same each time. With a sequence of six, a pattern will develop.

EVALUATION

When reviewing the tapes, here are some things to look for:

Address— Is the clubhead square to the ball? Are you set up exactly square to the target? Look to see if you regrip just prior to backswing.

Backswing — Is there a coil and a weight shift? At the top, is the shaft parallel to the ground and along the target line? Are your thumbs under the shaft?

Downswing — Does the club come straight down, or does it incorrectly come around to the ball? Does your right knee move left? Does your weight shift to your left side?

Impact — Is the clubhead square to ball and target? Have you hit down on the ball? Is your left side driving?

Finish — Are you balanced? Are you square to your target?

Aim the chip shot with the clubface only. You can't use your feet for aiming, because your stance is too open. The clubface should be set at a 90° angle to the target line for all chips. This is very important because the clubface should not change its angle at any time during the chip stroke. Except for the putt, the chip is the most targeted shot in golf.

Chip Stroke—Use your arms and shoulders primarily. Your hands are not extremely active, but neither are they stiff. If only your arms swing the club and there is no release of the clubhead with your hands, you are liable to hit behind the ball. If your ball is in heavy fringe grass, you will have to use a little more wrist action, along with a slightly more vertical swing. Here again, you simply hinge the wrists, but not nearly as much as for other shots.

With the club rising at impact, you don't sweep the ball—you hit down on it. Let the loft of the club you're using determine the resultant height of the shot.

The length of the backswing for the chip determines how hard, and therefore far, you will hit the ball. Here, your touch for the shot comes into play. Many golfers take too long a backswing for their chip shots. Then, realizing in mid-swing that it is too much swing, they slow the club down at impact.

I would rather see a shorter backswing with some firmness to it, producing a stroke with some acceleration to and through the ball. With your practice strokes, emulate the tempo of the swing you will be using for the shot itself.

THE "TEXAS WEDGE"

There will be times when you're in a position to play a standard chip, or even pitch, to the green but decide not to because your ball is sitting on very tight grass or even bare ground. Using a lofted club with such a lie often results in your hitting behind the ball—"chili-dipping" it, as the saying goes.

The safest club to use in this case is the putter, which has come to be known for this shot as the "Texas wedge." That's because to play the putter from off the green this way you must have very hard ground with very little grass to play over. And in Texas that is, or was, the case. Texans made the shot popular when they learned to use their putters to roll the ball through a lot of fringe grass.

The setup for this shot is the same as for a regular putt—because, basically, that's what the shot is. It is essential, of course, that the grass you are putting through to get to the green be very low and firm. Many golfers will play the "Texas wedge" through lush grass, and they almost invariably come up short of their target. I would also recommend that the shot not be used when there is a lot of undulation either in the fringe or the green. Use it only over relatively flat and low-cut, hard ground. This way it can be a very effective stroke-saver.

GOLF TIP

Here's a wet-weather rule you may not know: If your ball lands in a trap that has casual water, you get a free drop in the trap. However, if the trap is *filled* with water and you elect to drop out of the trap, there is a one-stroke penalty.

Using the "Texas wedge" is most helpful when your lie on long grass would make a normal chip shot risky. For these special situations, consider putting through to the green.

CHAPTER SEVEN

Putting

There is truth to the old golf adage, "Drive for show and putt for dough." In fact, more than 40% of all the strokes in every round of golf are made on the greens. It should come as no surprise then, that the difference between winning a tournament on the pro tour and finishing second, fifth, tenth, or out of the money, is almost invariably measured by how the putting goes.

One beautiful drive after another, each in the fairway and with good distance, can be wasted if you can't follow through with effective putting. What's more, good putting can make up for those times when you are not hitting the ball well off the tee or from the fairway. Good driving will never compensate for bad putting.

Even the best putters in the game, however, are not at their very best as consistently as you might think. During the early part of 1985 for example, Ben Crenshaw, always considered one of the best on the greens, had trouble even making the cut from week to week—because of his poor putting.

Putting skills tend to come and go. Some days, or even weeks, it seems that you can't miss a putt. Other times nothing falls in, even when the ball has been properly stroked. No one has yet explained the up-and-down nature of putting, which is one reason why it is the most idiosyncratic part of golf.

There are almost as many different putting styles as there are putter designs. Even so, there are some fundamental techniques that work for most golfers, or at least for those who have been the most consistently successful. This chapter covers those fundamentals. With them you will have a foundation from which you can add your own ideas and methods.

When you putt, your target becomes an exact spot either at the cup (for short putts) or a spot on a line through which you intend to have the ball roll. Focusing on this target from alignment through actual strokes is an important key to consistent putting.

STRATEGY

The purpose of a putt is to get the ball in the hole with a single stroke, especially from a distance of 12 feet or less. From this range you should make a high percentage of your putts. Outside that range, your odds of making the putt get proportionately worse. Your goal for longer putts should be to make the ball stop within a foot of the cup if it doesn't go in. As a result, the next putt should be just about impossible to miss.

As a rule of thumb, a putt of more than 12 feet should never go more than one foot past the hole. I can't overstress the goal of no more than two putts on the green. That's something that every beginner can achieve.

Using the principles of target golf is especially important in putting because you often need to aim the putter blade to a target that allows for green contour. Here, the target is the center of the cup because the green is level.

Consistency—In putting you want to develop a method that is as repeatable as possible. You want to hit the ball the same way as often as you can. When you can move the club along the same path at the same speed with great regularity, you can develop a feel for how hard to hit the ball for whatever distance you need. You will also be more consistently on target.

The golfer who most often putts the ball on the correct line and at the right distance is going to make the best score. Not all of his putts will go into the cup, but a reasonably high percentage will. And most important, there will be far fewer times when he'll need more than two putts.

One very important key to achieving this goal is to keep your body perfectly still throughout the entire putting stroke. This gives you the best chance of swinging the putter back and forth in the same path consistently. Other putting fundamentals follow.

PUTTING GRIP

A central purpose of the putting grip is to maintain control over the clubface so it does not change its angle relative to the ball at any time during the stroke. The angle of the clubface is set at address at 90°, or square, to the target line. The clubface should never deviate from that angle.

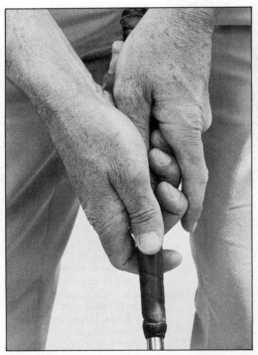

Here are two views of the reverse overlap. All of the fingers of the right hand are on the club handle. Your left index finger extends down to give a unified grip.

Reverse Overlap—The grip should also provide you with a sensitive touch for the distance you must hit the ball. The one I recommend is the *reverse overlap*. To take this grip, begin with the right hand. Place the handle of the club along the callus line and wrap the last three fingers around the handle. The index finger is positioned just as for full-swing shots—it is separated from the other three and forms a crook as if fingering a trigger.

You want to feel that you are holding the club in the fingers of your right hand. The primary function of your right hand is to control the distance of the putt. The fingers are the most sensitive parts of your hand, and the placement of your index finger increases club control.

Your right thumb should ride down the center of the handle.

The primary function of your left hand is to keep the putter blade on the same swinging path throughout the stroke, thus controlling the direction of the putt. In positioning your left hand, place the handle of the club between your thumb and pad so the handle runs nearly through the center of your palm. Your left thumb also runs down the middle of the handle.

The name *reverse overlap* refers to how the two hands connect to complete the grip. The reverse overlap I recommend extends the index finger of your left hand across all the fingers of your right hand, usually between the nails and middle knuckles.

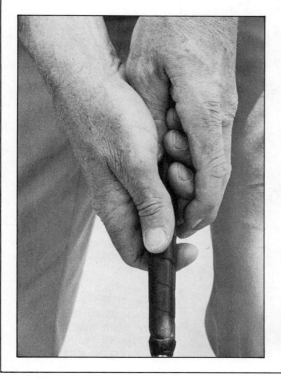

The Arnold Palmer variation of the reverse overlap makes the hands feel like one unit. Notice that two fingers of the left hand extend over the right.

Reverse-Overlap Variations—Some golfers will place the left index finger along the crevice formed by the little finger and third finger of the right hand. This is the exact opposite of the overlap grip used for full shots.

Other variations include placing the index and middle fingers of your left hand over the little finger and third finger of your right hand. Arnold Palmer uses this grip.

However you connect your hands in the putting grip—and it is simply a matter of what is the most comfortable for you—the back of your left hand should be facing directly toward the target. The back of your right hand should be facing directly away from it. Neither hand is twisted or turned. As a unit they are "square" to the target, just as the clubface is.

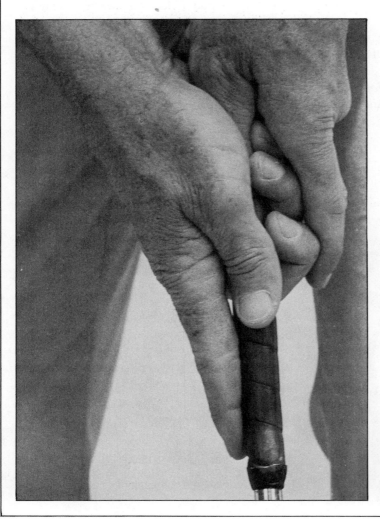

Some golfers prefer to hold the right index finger extended along the shaft. They claim that this promotes extra "feel" and control during the stroke.

GRIP PRESSURE

Your grip pressure should be relatively light, with the right hand a bit lighter than the left. I can't be any more specific than that about grip pressure because everyone has a different sense of his own strength, security, or sensitivity.

Obviously, you want to hold the putter firmly enough with both hands so the club is under control at all times. You don't want to grip it so tightly, however, that sensitivity is lost. Each golfer has to discover the happy medium between a grip that is too tight and one that is too loose.

Consistency—Whatever your individual grip pressure may be, it is essential that it remain constant throughout the stroke. This is a universal putting rule for all golfers, from beginners to pros. If grip pressure changes during the stroke, the angle of the clubface can change the pace of the stroke and make it uneven, resulting in a missed putt.

STANCE AND SET-UP

The putting stance and set-up are the most personalized things about putting. Though most golfers seem to prefer playing the ball off the left foot, which I think is best, there are good putters who play the ball in the middle of their stance. Some even play it off of the right foot.

Upswing Contact—The stance and set-up I recommend for putting is what you will see among the game's best players. It is designed to hit the ball when the clubhead is just past the bottom of its arch and beginning to rise. Thus, the ball is hit slightly on the upswing. When hit on the upswing, the ball tends to hug the ground more.

Just about every ball putted from longer than three or four feet will come off the ground a little when first struck because putters are made with a certain amount of loft—on average about 3°. You need that loft to start the ball rolling freely, but the more you can minimize loft, the more accurate your shot. Furthermore, a ball hit on the upswing is more likely to have overspin, which produces the most complete and accurate roll.

Play Off the Left Foot—The surest way to hit the ball on the upswing is to play it off the left foot. It can be an inch or two one way or the other relative to the left heel, but the essential positioning is off the left foot.

To find your own specific position determine where the bottom of your swing arc is. You do this by taking a few practice strokes and noting at what point the putter brushes the top of the grass. That point is the bottom of the swing arc. You then position the ball slightly forward of that point so you will hit the ball when the putter's blade is just beginning to rise.

Slightly Open Stance—Another facet of putting for which there are many variations is the angle of the feet relative to the parallel line. Some golfers like an open stance when putting—that is, the left foot is drawn back from the parallel line, and the toes are angled slightly toward the target.

Others prefer a closed stance, with the right foot drawn back from the parallel line. Then there are those golfers who keep the toes of both feet even with each other, on the

To hit the ball on the upswing of your putt, position yourself so the ball is approximately aligned with your left foot.

parallel line in the square position.

Of the three basic positions, the square and open stance are most commonly used. Tom Watson, an excellent putter, best exemplifies the square putting stance. Jack Nicklaus, one of golf's greatest putters, has always used a slightly open stance. With an open stance you are essentially facing the target, and so have a little better view of it. The open stance also allows your arms a little more leeway to swing through during the forward stroke.

A square stance, on the other hand, is more consistent with the way you hit all your full shots, and any way you can build consistency into your overall game is helpful. Also, the square putting stance tends to promote the kind of straight-back/straight-through putting stroke everyone should strive for.

Practice all of the stances described here and settle for the one that suits you best.

Weight Left for Stability—As I've said, it is important to good putting that your body remain absolutely still during the stroke. To help achieve that, place almost all (60%) of your body weight on your left foot and center your weight on your instep.

To further guarantee that your body is firmly braced for the stroke, kink your right knee toward your left leg so you feel a slight pressure on the inside of your right foot.

Arms Hang Naturally—The lower part of your body is firmly braced so it does not move during the stroke. That firmness should not go so far as to create tension, though especially in your upper body. To create a fine balance between tension and a too-relaxed state, bend over slightly at the waist and let your arms hang naturally—directly from your shoulder joints. If your arms are not stretched out in front of you so that your elbows lock, neither are they held so closely to your body that your elbows bend. Let your arms hang down in front of your body as if you were standing relaxed.

If you set your arms this way at address, your putter will be a direct extension of your arms; thus the correct distance between the ball and your feet will be determined automatically. If you stretch out your arms too far at address, the ball will be too far from

An important part of the proper putting stance is to let your arms fall naturally from your shoulders.

your feet, and you are likely to open the putter blade during the stroke. On the other hand, if your arms are in too close to your body, the ball will be too close to your feet and you are apt to "hood," or close the putter blade during the stroke.

By letting your arms hang naturally you create the proper posture for putting. If you're stretching your arms, you will bend too much at the waist or slump your shoulders. If you are up too close to the ball, you will be standing very erect, which creates tension. The best putting posture is the same as for all other shots—a straight back with a slight bend at the waist.

Be sure to keep both of your arms and elbows parallel to the line of putt and aligned in the same plane. In other words, your right elbow should not be higher or lower than your left elbow, nor should it be drawn back further. Have them on the same parallel plane to the line of putt. It may help to picture a rod going through each elbow and having that rod point on a parallel line from ball to target.

Eyes on the Ball—How you use your eyes in putting has a lot to do with the degree of success you will have. First of all, it is very important to have your eyes directly over the ball at address. For example, if you dropped a coin from between your eyes, it should fall onto the center of the ball.

If your eyes are positioned over a line inside the ball you will probably lean back from the ball. Conversely, if your eyes are on a line outside the ball, your body is likely to lean too far forward. In either case, it is very difficult to make a straight-back/straight-through stroke.

With your eyes directly over the ball, you will set your body in the correct balance. You will also have the proper angle to see if your putter blade is square to the target line.

Although both of your eyes are on a line directly over the ball, you actually look at the very back of it, which of course is where you want to hit it. Concentrating on the back of the ball increases your body's stability during the stroke. You must also keep your eyes on that point for a moment after the ball has been struck and is on its way. This assures that your head will not move during the stroke.

Gary Player once told me that a checkpoint he uses in putting is to imagine he is tapping a tack into the very back of the ball with each stroke. This image helps him make a solid hit—one that is firm and positive.

Hands Slightly Ahead—At address your hands should be slightly ahead of the ball. This position encourages a firm stroke with the blade moving along the target line. You might keep your hands even with the ball, but you definitely do not want your hands behind the ball at address because this tends to produce a loose, "wristy" stroke.

I recommend that you position your hands slightly ahead of the ball. Set up at the same time you place the clubhead behind the ball. If you set your clubface square behind the ball and later move your hands ahead, you will almost certainly change the angle of the clubface. It will probably open some and aim to the right of your target.

Drop a coin from between your eyes to determine if your stance has your eyes directly over the ball. You do if the coin hits the ball.

Try Gary Player's visualization technique of tapping a tack into the ball with the putter blade. It promotes a solid hit.

Getting the Blade on Target—Aligning the clubface so it is perfectly square to the target line is not as simple as it may seem. Because you are looking at the clubface from pretty high up and at a slight angle, you can deceive yourself. You should check periodically to see that you have aligned the clubface properly. Here are ways to do this:

1) Take your address position. Then, holding the club in place, step back behind the ball and see if the clubface is at the correct 90° angle to the target line.

2) On the practice green, place two clubs on either side of the ball parallel to the target line. Separate them just slightly wider than the length of your putter blade. Now, place your putter blade inside the space. It should be at a 90° angle, or square, to the target.

While you are in this set-up, you might also hit some putts to practice the straight-back/straight-through putting stroke. During your practice putts, your putter should not touch either of the clubs you have placed on the ground.

3) Have a friend stand behind you while you are putting to see whether you have the putter blade square to the target line during the address and the stroke.

PUTTING STROKE

In the most efficient and effective putting stroke, the lengths of the backswing and follow-through are identical. This kind of balance promotes a smooth, evenly-paced stroke.

The tendency among inconsistent putters is to produce a much longer backswing than follow-through, resulting in bad putts. Here's why: Instinctively the golfer realizes that if the length of the backswing is matched with an equally long follow-through, the ball will be hit too hard. To correct the problem, he slows down the stroke during the forward swing. The resulting club deceleration moves his head and body, changing the angle of the clubface. Not only is the direction of putts uncertain with deceleration, but also the speed of the ball is unpredictable. Therefore the golfer can never be sure how fast and how far the ball will roll.

Achieving a Balanced Stroke—I recommend that every golfer practice putting by first taking very short backswings and accelerating the clubhead through impact with the ball. Then you can gradually increase your backswing until you find the stroke length that suits the distance needed to get the ball into the hole. This way the entire stroke will eventually become smooth from start to finish.

Ideally, the putter head should be accelerating slightly at impact, but you shouldn't increase the speed consciously. Let it happen naturally, as it will if the lengths of the backswing and the follow-through are matched.

The length of the backswing determines how far you will hit the ball, provided the length of the follow-through is the same. This rule applies for putts of up to 35 or 40 feet. For longer putts, or for putts on slow grass, you may need to accelerate the stroke more than normal to generate enough clubhead speed. This is a better choice over a too-lengthy backswing and follow-through. Try to make the acceleration as smooth as possible.

Stroke Path—The best stroke path of the putter, as already suggested, is straight back and straight through. The club traces the target line. Naturally, the clubhead will raise slightly off the ground on the backswing and during the follow-through, but this should be a natural occurrence. Make no conscious effort to raise the club during the stroke. At the same time, do not force it to stay low to the ground either.

Moving Parts of the Stroke—Some golfers prefer to move the putter back and through with wrist action primarily and only just a bit of arm movement. Others swing the putter entirely with their upper arms and shoulders and do not let the wrists hinge at all. The latter method is currently the most popular and, in my opinion, the most effective technique.

Because hinging, or breaking, the wrists in the putting stroke is difficult to control consistently, the clubface is more likely to change its angle during the stroke—it may open or close if you hinge your wrists.

If, on the other hand, you stroke with the larger muscles of your arms and shoulders, you are going to be much steadier and more consistent. The clubface will almost invariably remain square throughout the stroke, and there will be much less chance of a deviation in the stroke path. You will get a sort of pendulum stroke that makes for natural and consistent putting.

For these reasons, you should learn to swing the putter back and through by moving just your shoulders and upper arms.

Starting the Stroke—In putting, as with all other golf strokes, it is important that you create a bit of motion while standing in place to create a smooth-flowing stroke. There are a number of ways to get this movement. Take your choice:

1) Use the forward press in which your hands and club handle are pushed slightly forward or ahead of the ball just before beginning the backswing. In effect, the forward press initiates the backswing.

2) Grip and re-grip the club a few times. That is, relax and tighten your fingers on the handle. This will also help you find the right grip pressure.

3) Take one practice stroke beside the ball, then step in and, with very little pause, hit the putt. Make sure your practice stroke simulates as nearly as possible the length of the stroke you intend to make.

4) Take your stance: Place the clubhead behind the ball, then in front of it. You might repeat this sequence twice before making the stroke.

5) Take your stance with the clubhead behind the ball. Look at the hole, and follow with your eyes the line of the putt right back to the putter blade. This is also a good way to check to see if the clubface is square to the target.

Whatever procedure you choose, do it every time you putt. That is the way to build consistency into your overall method. The more consistent you are in everything you do, the more you will follow an established pattern—and the more comfortable you will be. This translates in to a putting rhythm that produces a smooth stroke every time.

When practicing, step behind the ball while holding the putter where you originally aligned it. This way you can see if you have a tendency to aim the ball to the right or left.

Finding the Line of a Putt—A great many of the putts you play will break in one direction or another. That is, the path to the hole is not always straight. Often, the terrain tilts or banks, and you must allow for that in aiming and stroking the ball. If the ground along your line of putt banks down from right to left, or left to right, you must start the ball high enough on the bank so it will curve into the hole.

Some putts travel uphill or downhill, so there will be times when you have to make a putt that will go up or down and *also* break to the right or left.

When you play target golf, it helps to mentally draw the line you want the putt to travel.

There is a way to determine the "break" in the terrain you must putt over. To find out if there is a right-to-left or left-to-right bank, walk behind the ball, bend low and look along the ground *between your ball and the hole.*

To determine if the route is uphill or downhill, crouch down and look at the terrain from a position to one side or the other of your line of putt and about midway between your ball and the hole. You'll see the slope, if any.

Once you have discovered in what direction the ground banks, you must figure out how much you should allow for the break when you hit your putt. For the most part, you learn this through experience. No one can tell you just how high up on a bank you must hit the ball to make it curve into the hole.

Nor can anyone tell you how much harder you must hit a ball when it must go uphill, nor how gently when it must go downhill. It depends on the steepness of the hill, and how fast the green itself is running. A green with longer grass and a soft base will not run as fast as one that has shorter grass and a firm base.

Even so, there is one general rule that will help you judge how much break to allow on putts over banked terrain. That is, the faster the ball is rolling on sidehill putts, the less it will break.

Every Putt a Straight Putt—After you have looked over the terrain and decided at what point along the line of putt the ball will begin to curve toward the hole, note that spot. Then hit the ball toward it as though you were playing a straight putt. Essentially, this is *target putting*. The idea behind this is to insure that you make your same straight-back/ straight-through stroke.

The tendency among golfers putting over uneven ground is to make a stroke that matches the slope of the ground. That leads to poorly hit putts. The stroke should be no different from your normal putting stroke.

Here's one more important point in playing breaking putts: After deciding where and how much your ball will break, stick to your decision. Golfers often make one judgment when they are crouched behind their ball studying the terrain of the green. Then when they get into the address position, they look at the line from a different perspective and rethink the break. That almost always leads to a poorly hit putt.

Avoid this problem by making up your mind once and going through with it. If you happen to be wrong, so be it, but at least you will have made a solid stroke that will not interrupt your rhythm on subsequent holes.

THE "ART" OF PUTTING

The technical side of putting is plain and simple if you develop a consistent stroke. There is however, another side to this important shot—the "art" of putting. What follows are some thoughts on the "art" of putting that may help you to understand the difference between good putters and great ones.

Know Your Putter—Every putter has what is called a *sweet spot*—a point on the clubhead where balance is centered. This is the spot that should contact the ball because it produces the most solid and truest hit. The clubhead will not open or close at impact if you hit the ball with the sweet spot. The blade *will* turn, though, if you hit the ball off the physical centerpoint of the blade.

The sweet spot is usually in the middle of the blade of the putter or slightly in toward the shaft. Many putter manufacturers indicate the sweet spot on their equipment with some kind of mark—a groove or arrow on the top edge of the blade.

Even so, sometimes the manufacturer is off the mark. In this case, you have to determine the sweet spot for yourself. It's easy.

Suspend the putter in the air from its handle tip so it hangs straight down. Then, with a small coin, tap the clubface at various points where you think the sweet spot is. If the blade opens or closes and does not swing straight back, you have not hit the sweet spot. When the putter swings straight back and the blade stays square, you have found the sweet spot. If there is no mark at that point, put one there yourself with a small piece of tape, a bit of paint, or a small file cut.

Never Up, Never In—It goes without saying that a putt that does not reach the hole is never going to fall in. Yet many golfers fail to hit putts hard enough to get to the hole. They follow the old theory that says the ball should "die" in the hole, that is, you should hit the ball just hard enough to reach the cup. The premise is that a slow rolling ball has a better chance of curling into the cup than one rolling faster.

I don't believe it. This advice is the main cause of short putts. I think that you should hit every putt with the intention of sending it about 12 inches past the hole if it doesn't drop. That's what "getting it up to the hole" means. Remember, *never up, never in.*

Learn From Others—A good way to get a sense of how fast a green is running, breaking and sloping is to observe the shots of your playing partners. Keep your eyes open. It's free "advice" toward making better scores.

Visualize Your Putting Line—Get a visual image of the line on which you want to roll your ball. Start from the hole and "draw" that line all the way back to your ball.

Stay in the Present—Every putt is a brand-new experience. You must not think of putts missed—or made—earlier. Concentrate entirely on the putt at hand, and have a positive "I will make it" attitude.

Aim Within the Hole—When you are not sure of the line of a putt—if you just can't read the break—always aim into the hole, never outside of it. And on putts shorter than about four feet, never play the ball on a line outside the hole even when you can see the direction of the break clearly.

PUTTING CHECKPOINTS

1) Survey the line to determine if the putt is uphill, downhill or banked. Observe the play of the others in your group to help assess the speed and break of the green.

2) Align the clubface at a 90° angle to the target line.

3) Put most of your weight on your left foot, at a ratio of 60% left to 40% right.

4) Use the reverse overlap grip, with your left hand exerting a bit more pressure than your right hand. Keep overall grip pressure constant throughout the stroke.

5) Keep your eyes directly over the ball, or the target line, and concentrate on hitting the back of the ball.

6) Let your arms hang naturally at address, neither stretched out too far from your body nor in too close.

7) Make the length of your backswing the same as the follow-through. The length of the backswing determines how far you will hit the ball.

8) Hit the ball just as the club is beginning to rise during the forward swing. You can do this by playing the ball at a predetermined point off your left foot.

9) Make the stroke primarily with your shoulders and upper arms. Don't hinge your wrists. The putter blade travels along the target line both back and through.

Limit Your Keys—Almost every golfer will come up with a "key" thought for each round, usually a piece of technique such as the position of the hands at address, grip pressure or weight distribution. That is fine because having a single thought helps your overall concentration under pressure. But you should have only *one* thought, one *key*—and it should be as simple as possible. You don't want to be thinking about a lot of complicated techniques while putting.

PUTTING SUMMARY

So far, I have pointed out many things that you have to do in putting—grip and stance, aiming the clubface, judging the terrain. It may seem to be more than anyone can handle at one time, but the more you play the more these actions meld into one automatic stroke. In fact, once you have gone through all the pre-putt procedures, including the alignment of the clubface at a 90° angle to the target line, you should cast it all from your mind and think only of making a smooth, rhythmic stroke. In the final analysis, that's all you want. Technique and checkpoints are merely aids to getting the ball into the cup with as few shots as possible.

GOLF TIP

Here is a way to help you spot a fast green. With the grain, there will be shine to the grass. Against the grain, the grass will have a darker hue.

CHAPTER EIGHT

Trouble Shots

The shot I remember best from my career occurred on the 72nd hole of the 1978 Byron Nelson Classic. I had pushed my tee shot directly behind a tree, and when I got to the ball I saw that the low-hanging branches completely blocked my approach to the green.

I was looking for a way out of this mess, resigning myself to a bogie—at best. Then my caddie noticed that the wind, which was blowing quite hard, occasionally forced the guilty limb to momentarily blow clear of a direct line (in both direction and height!) to the green.

Visualizing nothing but that opening, I set up for my shot and waited for my caddie's go-ahead. The wind blew and my shot whistled through the opening just before it closed up again and landed safely in the middle of the green. Only my caddie and I knew what a great shot it was, but I'll never forget it.

In fact, probably the biggest thrill in golf is to successfully play a shot from a trouble spot that appears impossible to handle. A key, as always, is to pick out a target. It may not be the hole, or even the green, but it must be a part of your plan.

This chapter is devoted to giving you techniques for playing various trouble shots and giving you things to consider before playing them. If you apply some of these tips, I'm certain that before long you too will create a shot that you'll always remember.

EXPLODING OUT OF THE SAND

Sand traps have been part of golf ever since the game was invented in Scotland. The first sand traps were pits created by sheep that had burrowed down to get out of cold winds blowing across the links lands of Scotland. Those original sand traps were much harder to play from than today's if only because they were never raked smooth. Also, golfers didn't have the sand wedge in those days, a club invented by Gene Sarazen in the 1930s.

Even though the sand wedge has made the shot vastly easier, most golfers dread playing out of the sand. This is understandable. Sand shots are tough.

And knowing that old-time golfers had it tougher playing out of the sand doesn't help much. The sand shot still requires some special technique and knowledge, no matter how much better present conditions may be. It is essential to learn how to play basic sand shots. These include the "explosion" from a bunker beside a green, and the long sand shot from a fairway bunker.

About the Explosion Shot — The explosion shot is played from sand traps beside greens. The distance you can hit the ball is generally less than 40 yards. It is called an explosion, because the club hits into the sand behind the ball with the force of the "exploding" sand moving the ball. In fact, the clubhead never touches the ball — it moves under it.

The sand wedge is designed specifically for the explosion shot. The main features of the club are its wide sole, angled flange, and heavy weight. Because of the way the flange is angled, the back of the club hits the sand first during the downswing. This prevents the leading edge of the club from digging too sharply into the sand.

Before the sand wedge was invented, golfers played out of bunkers with conventional #8 or #9 irons, which had (and still have) a very sharp leading edge and narrow sole. It was very difficult for even the game's best players to consistently skim under the sand with these clubs. More often than not, the sharp leading edge dug too deeply and the ball did not get out of the bunker. Instead, some players tried to "pick" the ball out without touching the sand, but that was an even more delicate shot. It was almost impossible if the ball was settled in a furrow, or simply buried in soft sand. With the sand wedge, you can play the ball from any kind of lie.

Even so, the sand wedge is not foolproof. You can hit the ball first or dig into the sand too deeply. There is a definite technique for playing the explosion shot correctly.

Address—The address position for the explosion is not unlike the address position described for the short pitch shot. Your stance is open, the left foot pulled back from the parallel line four to five inches for the average-distance shot.

If there is a particularly short distance between you and the hole, open your stance a few inches more to encourage a more vertical swinging plane. In other words, the more you open your stance, the more sharply you will hit down into the sand. The more sharply you hit down, the less distance you will get with the shot.

Open the clubface at address proportionate to how much you open your stance. For the standard explosion shot the face is slightly open, aimed about five feet to the right of your

EXPLOSION SHOT
1) Set up with a balanced stance, with slightly more weight on your left side and the clubface slightly open.

2) Stance should aim a bit to the left. The swing path should be parallel to the stance.

target. You never play a standard explosion shot with the clubface closed or aimed to the left of your target.

Take a slightly wider stance than normal for the explosion shot because you want very little body movement in the swing. You should also dig your feet into the sand to get solid footing, but this does not mean you have to bury them as many golfers do. Just move your feet around until they won't move freely—that's deep enough.

As you get your footing, be aware of the texture and depth of the sand. This is the only opportunity you will have to get this sense, or feel, of the stuff before you hit the shot. Remember, it's a penalty stroke to touch the sand with your club before you swing at the ball. You must hold the clubhead above the sand at the address.

Weight Distribution—For the explosion shot, your weight should be distributed about 60% to the left and about 40% to the right. Having the weight more to the left encourages a vertical swinging plane making you hit downward into the sand. It will also prevent your falling back onto your right side during the swing. You definitely want to have most of your weight on your left side at all times during this swing.

Ball Position—Play the ball inside your left heel, or on your instep, much as you do for the standard pitch shot. You don't want the ball too far forward in your stance because you will hit too far behind it.

Hands—At address your hands should be about even with the ball. Maintain the same good posture you use for all of your other shots—back straight and a slight bend at the waist.

Swinging—I don't want to put too much emphasis on hitting behind the ball for the explosion shot. Golfers usually misunderstand and hit too far behind. Generally aim to hit about an inch-and-a-half into the sand behind the ball. Keep your eye on the point in the sand where you want to make contact. Do not look at the ball.

Your swing will be more vertical—more up and down—than for standard shots. The swinging plane should occur naturally as the result of the address position, not as a forced or manipulated movement.

By the same token, neither should you try to swing the club outside on the backswing, that is, away from your body. You will probably hear that advice from other golf teachers or read it in other golf books. I urge you to ignore it. Here's my advice: The backswing for the explosion shot should be exactly the same as for standard shots.

Right-Hand Release—The most common error I have found among golfers in playing the explosion shot is not releasing the right hand in the downswing. They are afraid of hitting the ball first and sending it over the green or digging too deeply into the sand and not getting the ball out at all. Thus, they pull their arms forward and push their bodies backward. The results are often what they were hoping to avoid. They hit too far behind the ball and leave it in the bunker, or they *belly* it—hit the ball instead of sand and send it over the green.

Both problems are eliminated almost entirely if you release your right hand during the downswing. One way I've helped golfers release the right hand is to have them set as their

3) Look at that part of the sand you want to hit through. It's about 1-1/2 inches behind the ball.

goal to *get the clubhead under the ball and through the sand*. Don't think of anything other than getting the clubhead through the sand. That advice seems to help golfers make the shot properly.

The release of the right hand for the explosion shot is exactly the same as discussed in chapter 3, which covered the downswing. It comes as a rotation of the both hands—the two are a unit—but you *feel* that the right hand is the dominant force.

How deeply you dig into the sand with the clubhead depends on how much right-hand release you have in the shot. Odd as it may sound, the more you release the right hand, the less you will dig the club into the sand. Instead you will "spank" the sand with the club and take all the sand away within a two-inch radius around the ball. With a good explosion shot the "divot" is fairly shallow.

4) Release of hands is over, not under.

Calculating Distance—Normally, a ball exploded out of the sand will not have much backspin. Ideally, the ball will land softly and roll about a couple of feet forward. Calculate that into how hard you want to hit the ball for the distance you need.

With the explosion shot, just as with putting, the length of the backswing determines how far you will hit the ball. The longer the backswing, the farther the ball will travel. This is true only if you complete the swing with a full right-hand release and drive the club completely through the sand. You must follow through with this shot just as you do with shots from the grass.

SPECIAL SAND CONDITIONS

The technique described here is for an explosion shot from "normal" sand of medium density—not too thick or heavy and not too powdery or light. However, not all sand is like that.

Wet or Hard-Packed Sand—After a rain, or after a period of exceptional wind when a lot of sand has been blown out of the bunker, you will be playing off a hard-packed surface. The club is not going to penetrate the sand easily, requiring an altered technique.

5) The swing ends with a balanced finish.

You will want a sharper cutting edge to get the club under the ball. In this case you must square the clubface of your sand wedge.

All of the other mechanics of the swing are the same, but with the blade squared you will get the sharper leading edge of the club into play.

Soft Sand—When the sand is softer, deeper, and heavier than normal, you must open the face of the sand wedge more than usual. Here again, the mechanics of the swing remain the same, only the angle of the clubface is different.

Playing the "Plugged" Ball—Sometimes a ball will land in a sand trap and "plug" its own hole. Usually, you can see only the top half of the ball. The problem here is how to get the clubhead under the ball. You need a much sharper leading edge than you have on your sand wedge.

The solution is to use your pitching wedge. Square the face at address, and *hit the back edge of the crater* the ball is sitting in. The swing should be a little more vertical than usual and, in this case, you can't expect to have a follow-through. You want to swing down with enough force to extract the ball.

Don't expect to get this shot close to the hole. You can control only direction and the

**PLAYING THE
PLUGGED BALL**
1) To hit a plugged ball, align the clubface square to slightly closed. Have your weight more on your left side.

ball invariably has a lot of roll after landing. Your main goal with this shot is to get the ball onto your target, the green.

FAIRWAY BUNKER SHOT

The first thing you must understand about playing out of a fairway bunker is that it is just like any shot you play from the grass. *You must hit the ball first.* That is difficult, mainly because your footing is insecure, and because golf rules forbid your touching the club on the ground behind the ball. The best way to insure that you will hit the ball first is to assume the proper address position for playing the fairway bunker shot.

Address—Almost everything I discuss about the address position is designed to get you to hit the ball first:

1) Play the ball more toward the center of your feet. It should still be placed left of center, but not as much as for normal shots.

2) Distribute your weight about 55% on your left side and 45% on your right side.

2) The resulting downward blast will not allow for much follow-through. It's essentiall to stay down through the shot.

3) Dig your feet firmly into the sand, but no more than for the explosion shot. You're going to be making a full swing, which requires some lower-body movement, including your feet.

4) Choke down on the club proportionate to how deeply your feet sink into the sand. When your feet go below the level of the ball, you must adjust the length of the club accordingly. Club length should not be too long; that could cause you to hit behind the ball.

5) Keep the clubface square and your hands in their normal position relative to the ball. This position should be even with the ball, or just slightly ahead of it.

Club Selection—Be conservative in club selection. The most important factor here is that you will probably have to get the ball above the lip of the trap, a problem you do not face with a fairway shot. If your ball is especially close to the lip, you will have to use a club with enough loft to guarantee getting the ball over it even if that club is not enough to get you to the green. Your first job is to get the ball out of the bunker.

As a rule of thumb, try this: If you think a #6 iron has enough loft to clear the lip, use a #7 iron. If the #8 is what you think you need, use the #9—and so on.

Of course, if your ball is sunk into the sand of a fairway trap, none of the above applies.

You must play an explosion back into the fairway and try to make up for the lost stroke with a good putt after you reach the green.

Swing Easier—Since all of the address positions described here are meant to give you stability in the sand for a full swing, it is best to use a three-quarter swing. Restrict your backswing to travelling three-quarters of its normal path. This will help you maintain both swing control and balance. You don't want to take any chance of leaving the ball in the trap.

UPHILL AND DOWNHILL SHOTS

In playing off of uneven lies, either in a sand trap or on grass, the address position is most important. The swing itself for various unlevel lies is the same as for normal shots. That is, you should *feel* that the swing is normal. Although the swing will be somewhat different in each case, *it is a natural result of the address position you will have taken.*

But no matter how sound your address position may be for any of these shots, there is always the chance of your falling out of balance and the shot going off target. You can guard against this by applying the following principles for playing off of unlevel lies. First, slow the tempo of your swing somewhat. Second, take a three-quarter swing.

If you apply these principles, however, you will need to use one more club than the one you had planned to use for the shot, or the club you would have used for a lie on level ground. If you had selected a #6, for example, use a #5 to compensate for the slowed tempo and the three-quarter swing.

Uphill Shot—In an uphill shot you want to make your body conform to the slope of the ground so that you are, in essence, simulating a level lie with your body at a 90° angle to the target line. To do this going uphill put more of your body weight on your right leg. Your body will actually be tilting to the right, just as the ground is.

Now you can swing the club naturally along the lay of the land and make it move through impact with the ball just as though you were playing off level ground. If you stand with your weight evenly distributed, you will, in effect, be inclined too much to the left. The club may never get through impact with the ball if the slope is especially steep, and the shot will not have the power it should.

Otherwise, the address position is the same as for normal shots. Play the ball at the same spot off of your left heel. Keep you hands even with the ball.

When playing uphill, you are going to hit the ball higher than you would usually. Thus, it will not go as far as it would normally, and you should take one more club than you would ordinarily use for the distance. For example, you would hit a #5 iron if normally you would select a #6 iron.

Downhill Lie—With a downhill lie you reverse your weight distribution. You put more weight on your left leg so you can swing the club back without hitting the ground sloping up behind you.

Of all the uneven lies, this is probably the most difficult on which to get proper loft. Many golfers try to lift the ball into the air by manipulating the club with their hands and body. It never works. Trust your address position to help you make solid contact with the ball, and the thrust loft of the club itself to get the ball into the air.

You should know that regardless of how well you make contact with the ball, the flight is going to have a lower-than-usual trajectory. To compensate for this use a club with a loft higher than the club required for the distance. For example, if the distance requires a #6 iron, use a #7 iron for its increased loft. You will still get the distance of the #6 iron because the nature of the lie reduces the loft of the club being used.

You should also play the ball back a little more toward the center of your feet for downhill lies. The steeper the hill, the farther to the right you play the ball.

Because shots from this lie have a low trajectory, you may have trouble carrying a sand trap or water hazard in a direct line to your target. On shorter shots, say from 125 yards and in, this shouldn't be a serious problem. But for longer shots I advise you to aim away from the trap or water.

Another thing to consider is that balls hit from a downhill lie usually have more run. You will have to compensate for this. Perhaps the best way to compensate is to use a three-quarter swing and to slow the tempo of your swing slightly.

Sidehill Lie with Feet Above the Ball—Because you will have a tendency to fall forward on shots with a sidehill lie with your feet above the ball, an easy swing is essential. For this lie, flex your knees a little more than usual at address. This will help give you better balance and the ability to maintain it during the swing.

Balls played from a sidehill lie generally go to the right. If you stay with the shot, keep your balance, and don't try to power the ball. It will not drift very much to the right. As a rule, however, it is a good idea to aim a few yards to the left of your target.

If the slope is especially severe, you will have to swing the club back on a path away from your body to avoid hitting the ground with it. In this case, the ball will probably go well to the right. You must adjust your aim accordingly.

The distance the ball travels on sidehill lie shots is usually what it is for normal shots.

Sidehill Lie with Feet Below the Ball—When the lie is on the side of a hill and your feet are below the ball you will tend to hunch your body forward at address and get too close to the ball. If you do, it will be difficult to swing the club to conform with the slope of the ground. You will make a swinging plane that is too vertical.

The first thing you want to do with this shot is choke down on the grip an inch or so. This makes the club the same length it would be for a level lie, allowing you to stand a normal distance from the ball. You should also use less knee flex at address. This will make you feel as if you are standing tall at the ball.

Balls hit from the sidehill lie where your feet are below the ball generally fly from right to left. Do not try to prevent this by opening the clubface. Just aim a little farther to the right to allow for the abnormal flight pattern.

Here again, the distance you get from this lie is about what it is for normal shots.

Playing the Extra Low Shot—When you have to hit a ball under the low-hanging branches of a tree, do not hit down on the ball with a sharply vertical swing. The more you hit down on a golf ball, the higher it will go in the air.

To play the intentional low shot, choose a club with very little loft. It may be a #3 iron, even if the distance to the hole calls for a #7 iron. You compensate for this club selection with the force of your swing. It is crucial to make an easy swing.

Choke down on the grip. Play the ball farther back in your stance—at least in the middle, and in some cases right of center—and concentrate more body weight on your left side.

Your backswing plane is normal, but in the downswing you want to make a little more of a lateral slide to the left with your hips. You compensate for this by releasing the right hand fully into the shot. Think of making contact with the top half of the ball. Keep your hands low in the follow-through.

Of course, if you have to keep the ball very low and your ball is also down low in the grass, you will need to hit down on the ball to move it out. In this case, don't try to get under the branches. Try to find a clearing and play through it, even if that will not get you closer to the hole. Your first job, as with most "trouble" shots, is to get the ball out to where you can play a normal shot.

Playing the Extra-High Shot—To get a ball extra high over a tall tree or bush that's in your line, you want to hit down on the ball with a more vertical blow. There is more to the technique, however, than that.

At address, play the ball more forward in your stance—perhaps an inch or so more. In your swing do not move your body laterally. Keep your knees still. Do not fall backward and try to lift the ball up, a common fault. Keep your body relatively still, and make a full release of your hands into impact. You want to think of hitting the very bottom of the ball. As the great British champion Henry Cotton once put it, "Try to nip the little feet off the ball."

GOLF TIP

When hitting into the wind, position yourself so so the ball is farther back in your stance than normal. Use the next higher club than you would ordinarily and swing easy. Remember that the feel of wind in your face creates tension, and the desire to swing harder. Don't. The harder the swing, the higher the ball's flight — exactly what you don't want.

CHAPTER NINE

Tips & Techniques For Play & Practice

After years of teaching golf I have learned that it is sometimes necessary to say the same thing three or four different ways before the idea is understood. I don't mind that—it is part of the challenge of my work. But I think that students should also understand that and be patient with their instructor and with themselves. The learning process is never as straightforward or fast as we would like.

I've taught people who needed something more than an explanation to understand and perform a fundamental of the swing. They needed what can be called *body language*—an unusual exercise that brings home the message. I cover some of the most successful of those unusual exercises in this chapter.

Here, I also offer tips on techniques that didn't quite fit into the flow of the preceding chapters. They go a bit beyond fundamentals. These tips are for the experienced golfer who is beyond the basics and is ready to get into some of the more unusual, if not esoteric, facets of the game.

Finally, you will find some advice on how to practice, and some drills designed to prevent poor swings and create better ones.

THE GOLFER WHO COULDN'T SWING DOWN

I had a student once who was a fairly good player with a strange swinging problem. He would get to the top of his backswing and be unable to start the club down. He would move his body forward, but the club would stay behind, causing a sort of "stutter."

My assistant and I tried all sorts of things to get him out of this bad habit. We figured that if he kept his weight back on his right side he could start the downswing, but he couldn't do that.

As a last resort, we came up with a gimmick. We had him put his left foot on a driving-range-ball basket. This angled his body well to the right and prevented his moving it to the left. He began hitting balls with his left foot up on the basket and, lo and behold, he started his downswing properly and began hitting fine shots.

He finally got the feel of staying back on his right side and releasing the club from the top of the backswing. He started doing it correctly even without the helpful basket. His "stutter" disappeared permanently.

THE LADY WHO KEPT REGRIPPING

Several years ago I had a woman student who continually hit a "duck-hook"—the ball curved very sharply to the left and traveled only a few feet above the ground. The first thing I tried was to weaken her grip by having her turn her left hand more to the left.

This didn't help. The clubface was still closed at the top of her backswing and, of course, at impact with the ball. In short she kept duck-hooking.

I finally realized that she was regripping the club. She would start out at address with a proper grip, but just as she started her backswing her left hand would twist to the right into the strong position. This closed the clubface at the top of the backswing and caused the duck-hook.

Even though I described the problem and she understood it, she couldn't stop regripping. She needed a new procedure, something different to think about to break that destructive habit. I had her begin each swing by taking her correct grip and holding the club up in front of her about waist high. She then dropped it down behind the ball and began her swing. End of the re-gripping. Her shots began to go high and straight.

STRIKE INTO THE BALL

A student of mine couldn't seem to get the idea of how to shift his weight back to the left side in the downswing. He would spin his body sharply to the left and fall away from the ball.

To give him the feel of shifting his weight to his left side, I borrowed from baseball. I had him stride about four inches to the left with his left foot on the downswing. It is the same thing a baseball batter does when he hits the ball.

I've used this drill many times since, with good results. If you've played any baseball at all, you should be able to pick up the pointer. After hitting some balls with the stride, you can go back to hitting in the conventional way. You should then "feel" the weight shift to the left.

PRACTICE DRILL: GETTING CORRECTLY ALIGNED

One of the most common faults among golfers is alignment at address. Almost invariably they aim at least 30° to the *right* of their targets. I seldom see golfers aiming too much to the left. The real problem is that they usually don't realize it. And even pointing out the problem is not enough to correct it.

When I give a lesson I often place two clubs on the ground—one showing the aim of the clubface, the other the direction in which the student's feet are pointed. When the student steps back to see, he is amazed to note how far off he actually has aimed.

Your eyes can fool you in the address position. Try this procedure for yourself, with a club on the ground showing you where you are actually aiming. Do it regularly on the practice range. By improving your alignment you will improve your swing—every time.

PRACTICE DRILL: GETTING EXTRA YARDAGE

There are times when you really can use an extra 10 yards or so with a driver shot. It may get you close enough to the green to give you a good chance for a birdie or par. Or, it may allow you to out-drive an opponent for competitive pleasure or psychological advantage. Whatever the reason, there are many things golfers do wrong trying to hit the ball farther.

One is to tighten grip pressure, which in turn causes all your muscles to tighten. Another is to stand farther back from the ball. A third is to speed up the backswing by using your arms primarily.

Tightening grip pressure, which consequently tightens muscles elsewhere in your body, will reduce your flexibility. And without flexibility you have no power potential. So, as you can see, that is counterproductive.

If you stand back farther from the ball, you put your swing out of the normal groove. And, if you think about it, you'll realize that anything can happen as a result of that.

Speeding up you backswing by using your arms too much will prevent your body from coiling properly. This may cause you to lose your balance, resulting in a loss of timing, rhythm, and flow—and a loss of power.

Here are the keys to hitting the ball farther:

1) Keep *right-hand grip pressure* as light as possible. Stand tall at the ball.

2) In the backswing, emphasize a coiling of the left shoulder as the club starts back. This will control the tendency to let your arms run away from your body.

3) To maintain good balance, brace your right knee as your left shoulder begins to coil. Basically this means placing some pressure on the inside edge of your right foot.

4) Release your hands from the cocked position at the very start of the downswing. Keep the *swing* going. Do not hit at the ball. Your intention to hit the ball farther should take over in the downswing, not the backswing. It's natural to think that you must swing the club faster to hit the ball farther. You do, but *only in the downswing*. If you swing too quickly in the backswing you will not make a complete body coil. If you don't make that coil, you will end up *hitting* at the ball instead of swinging through with rhythm and balance.

PRACTICE DRILL: PUT YOUR BACK TO THE WALL

Many golfers take the club back too quickly to the inside and end up with a swinging plane that is too flat. That is, the club is well below the shoulders at the end of the backswing.

A good way to practice making a more upright swing is to take a stance with your back to a wall. Halfway into the backswing, the club should be parallel to the wall. From this point on it should travel upward to complete the backswing *without hitting the wall*.

After practicing this for a few minutes, take some full swings away from the wall. Your swing should be more vertical.

PRACTICE DRILL: FOR THE WHIP

If you have trouble starting the club down from the top of the backswing, try this exercise. Put a piece of ribbon on a golf shaft that has no clubhead. If the ribbon pops on the downswing, you are releasing your hands correctly. If you are not releasing, blocking your hand action, or flipping your hands too soon from the top, the ribbon will only flutter.

Pop the ribbon for a good release of your hands.

PRACTICE DRILL: STOPPING A SPIN OUT

If you tend to turn your left side too sharply and quickly to the left in the downswing, you are "spinning out." This usually causes you to lose your balance. Typically you will fall back on the right leg and get a poor release of the clubhead. You may either slice or badly hook the ball. I have a drill for preventing spin out that encourages the correct release of the club.

On the practice tee, place your right foot directly behind your left foot and point your right heel straight up. This forces you to keep your weight in balance when you hit balls.

Start with a few practice swings; then try some long chip shots from this position. Next you might hit some short iron shots. The idea of the drill is to take your body out of the swing, and of course, encourage a release of your hands to get the ball going.

After a few minutes of this drill, take your normal stance and hit some shots. You should find yourself releasing the clubhead and not twisting or spinning your body too soon.

PRACTICE DRILL: HANDKERCHIEF TRAINING

A drill used for years by pros and amateurs to ensure a good coil of the left shoulder in the backswing is worth reviewing here. Put a handkerchief or glove under your left arm and hit full golf shots without letting the handkerchief fall out.

To prevent the handkerchief from falling you must keep your left arm against your left side. This encourages your arms and shoulders to coil as a unit in the backswing.

This drill is also very good for learning to make a complete hand release, which is mirrored in the follow-through. Because you do not want the handkerchief to fall, in the follow-through you will not want your arms to get away from your body. This forces you to use more hand release than arm swing.

This swing will feel restricted, but after hitting a few balls you will increase your shoulder coil. Coiling is the only way to get the club away without letting the handkerchief fall.

PRACTICE DRILL: DROWNING THE DREADED SHANK

The most devastating shot in golf is the *shank,* which happens with iron shots. When you shank, you strike the ball with the hosel of the clubhead, that part of the clubhead that joins the shaft. This creates a shot that squirts directly to the right.

Fear of shanking lurks in the heart of any golfer who has hit one. This fear often creates *more* shanks, and it may become as much a mental as a mechanical problem.

The basic cause of shanking is failing to release the club properly in the downswing. This, in turn, is the result of other factors. It can come from spinning your left side too sharply to the left, from rushing your arms forward too quickly, or from moving your left side too far ahead of the ball in the downswing. In all cases, your hands will be unable to properly release the club, thus forcing the clubhead away from your body and toward the ball. The ball is then struck by the hosel.

To eliminate shanking I teach golfers to return to the fundamentals of a sound golf swing. I especially check to see that they are making as full a turn as possible in the backswing. This is especially important with the shorter irons, which seem to be the clubs most often shanked. The reason is simple: The backswing is shorter with these clubs and the turn more restricted.

Shanking can also result from tension in your hands, which often causes your arms to rush forward in the downswing. Your hands do not release properly because they are tense, or because the speed of the swing does not give them a chance.

Related to both problems is an overuse of your shoulders in the downswing. This creates an exaggerated outside-to-in swinging plane in which the clubhead is thrown well away from your body.

The best cure for shanking is to start the downswing *in place.* That is, start the club back to the ball with a vertical motion of your hands that gets them to release very soon in the action. Don't add any other body movement—just a release of your hands. That release, however, is not a flip of the wrists. Instead it's like the motion of flinging and releasing a Frisbee.

PRACTICE DRILL: ANOTHER TYPE OF RELEASE

There are a lot of ways to learn how to release the club at the start of the downswing. Here is another way that involves using your right index finger. Place it down the side of the club's handle but grip normally otherwise. Now hit shots.

This finger position gives you leverage to work the clubhead forward. The goal is to be pointing directly at the target with your index finger when you finish your follow-through. Your fingernail should be on the side of the shaft, not on the bottom or top.

Start this drill with chip shots and work up to longer shots made with a three-quarter swing. Do not hit the ball with a full swing. When you go back to your normal grip, the index finger of your right hand should be in the hook, or trigger, position.

PLAYING TIP: OVERCOMING INSECURITY

Every golfer gets into a situation during a round when he has to hit an especially good shot. If this moment occurs during tournament competition, you may feel panicky and insecure.

I am very familiar with the feeling myself. It is not restricted to amateur golfers. I recall in my rookie year on the pro tour leading a tournament by one stroke with only nine holes to play. The tension was building to the point where I had trouble getting the club started into the backswing. It wouldn't move.

What do you do under these circumstances? How can you hit a respectable shot? I've found that tension results from thinking more about results than the mechanics of the shot. What you need to do is develop a visual image of a successful shot. If you don't have a positive target image, panic and tension will surface and prevent a normal swing.

The way to overcome anxiety and insecurity is used by every well-coached athlete under pressure. Go back to the fundamentals of execution. Bury the tension under the security blanket of good habits:

1) Get a visual image of a successful shot. Think and see positively.

2) Decide exactly what you want to do with the shot before you get into the address position. *Don't change your mind*.

3) Be sure to go through your normal pre-shot routine all the way up to the final address position.

4) Think of swinging the club away from the target on the backswing, and to the target on the follow-through. Do not think of specific moves, such as turning the hips. Trust your instincts.

PLAYING TIP: CHIP LIKE A PUTT

If you are having trouble getting any consistency with chip shots from just off the edge of the green, try playing the shot like a putt. At address, point your elbows out to the sides to eliminate "wristiness." Use this technique only for short chips that do not require a lot of loft.

PLAYING TIP: SWING AT THE SAND SHOT

People who are afraid of sand shots tend to freeze at inopportune moments during the swing, and make short, punching jabs at the ball.

There is a better way. Use the power of your imagination. Imagine hitting a full smooth shot while trying to hit slightly behind the ball. Picture yourself with a fine, high follow-through. You'll be pleased, and surprised, to see the ball pop out nicely onto the green rather than flying over it.

PLAYING TIP: WARM-UP PRACTICE

A common error made by the average golfer who goes out to hit a few practice balls before a round is to start hitting full shots with the driver. You'll never see a pro or good amateur golfer do that. It is a good way to pull a muscle or strain your wrists.

It's much better to loosen your muscles gradually, including your hands. Begin by hitting a few short pitch shots. Don't even worry about aiming at anything—merely try to make good contact with the ball. As you begin to loosen, you can move up to longer irons and take careful aim to assure good alignment. End the session with the driver.

I also recommend hitting a few soft pitches or chips and to practice some putts on the practice green to restore sensitivity to your hands. Remember, you've hit a lot of balls in fairly rapid sequence, much more than you do on the golf course. Your hands need some time to recover from the pounding.

CHAPTER TEN

Children & Golf

I am often asked how to start a child in golf. The ideas presented here have worked well for me. I hope they do for you too.

STARTING

Even though every child develops at a different pace, mentally and physically, I think that a child can start at any time to hit a ball around the yard.

Even so, formal instruction should not begin before the age of nine. Children have short attention spans and are not likely to benefit from disciplined instruction before then. A great way for children to learn how to swing a golf club is to have them watch the likes of Jack Nicklaus or Tom Watson on television. Encourage them to mimic and imitate those swings. Children are natural imitators.

EQUIPMENT

It is very important for children to have clubs that fit. If the club is too long or heavy, the child won't be able to hit the ball and will quickly lose interest. Teaching pros often have odd clubs that can be cut down to the correct length and weight.

GRIP

Once children are properly fitted with clubs, start them off with the grip. I would not try to be too exacting with the grip at first. Keep in mind that the child has fun when he is swinging at the ball, not when he is constantly being told to correct his grip.

The most important part of teaching grip and address is to make sure the clubface is square to the ball. This will insure a long straight shot when the child does make contact. Too often I see a child make a good swing with the clubface either too closed or too open. The ball doesn't go anywhere.

To teach a child how to hold the club, ask him to "shake hands" with the club with both left and and right hands. To give the child better leverage, let him spread his hands slightly.

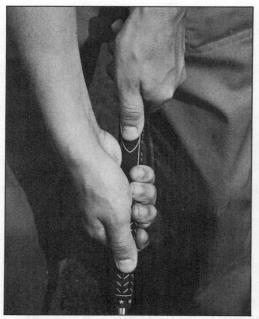 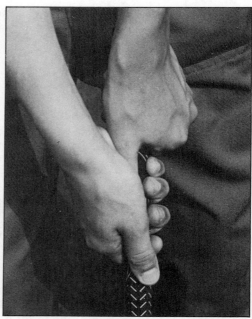

A young child's grip should have hands split apart for good leverage (left). As the child progresses and gets older, move the hands closer together (right).

SWING

Once the child takes his grip, he is ready to take a good hard swing at the ball. To do this he must have a strong balanced stance so he will maintain his balance during the swing. I recommend that the feet be set shoulder-width apart, with a slight flex in the knees and the right foot perpendicular to the target line. Never let the child forget about the target. He must learn from the start that golf is a target game. Always have him hitting at a target.

When teaching the swing, start with a "mini" swing. Get the child hitting the ball with

Have the child set his feet shoulder-width apart. Flex knees slightly for good balance.

Lay the club down along the parallel line to help the child align his body properly.

a short backswing and follow-through, much like a putting motion. As the child begins to hit the ball solidly, gradually allow him to take bigger swings.

It is difficult for a youngster to lift the club into the proper position at the top of the backswing, so let him swing away from the ball low and short (waist height). Then emphasize following through to the target. It is important to keep the backswing short at first—the swing is simpler and easier to repeat. As the child gets stronger, the length of his backswing will increase.

An image that helps me to describe the mini swing to a child is to tell him to reach back to shake hands with someone behind him and then to turn through impact to shake hands with someone in front of him.

Keep in mind that you want the child to make a mini weight shift to the right foot as the swing starts. Through impact he should shift that weight onto the left foot. Have the child roll his left ankle to the right as he makes the backswing. On the downswing, have him roll his right ankle to the left. This will create a natural flowing movement of weight during the swing.

A good way to get a child to make a correct swing is to have him identify with the correct finish position. A good finish position is a result of a good swing. If the child can

For beginners, the backswing should be short.

Swinging to a good balanced finish is important. A good exercise is to have the child swing to the finish without a backswing until the finish is correct.

see and then imitate a good finish position, he will probably hit a good shot. Try actually placing the child in the correct finish position—body turned fully to face the target, with all the weight on the left foot and both hands over the left shoulder.

FUN

Enjoying golf is a prime concern. The more children enjoy it, the more they will practice. A child needs to have success early on, so devise some easy and fun games. For example, you might invent a close-to-pin contest and allow the child multiple chances. Another way to make things easier for the child is to tee the ball up on every shot, even short irons. Once the child is consistently hitting the ball off the tee you can let him try hitting off grass.

Again, keep the learning fun. Don't give too many technical thoughts. Make up new games and remind the child that he is only competing against himself. Avoid pitting children against each other early on. If a child can learn basic mechanics, he will have a much easier time of golf when he grows up, and he will have a basis for playing a game that can provide a lifetime of fun.

CHAPTER ELEVEN

Practicing Target Golf

At the driving range, most golfers get a bucket of balls and hit away for 10 to 20 minutes. But it's my studied opinion that there is a better way. In fact, each practice session should have a planned procedure, a target, in which you work on specific parts of your game. If time is short, then cover each aspect briefly, but do practice all of the things discussed here.

Ideally, you should spend 90 minutes at the driving range. In this chapter, I've assumed 90 minutes and have dedicated a certain number of minutes to allocate to each part of your game.

Ben Hogan provides the best reason for this style of practice. He said, "The more I practice, the luckier I get." What Ben really was saying was that proper practice creates muscle memory, strengthens the swing and develops feel for the many kinds of approach shots required in any round of golf.

HAVE A PLAN

Because I recommend starting with the pitching wedge, I'll use this part of the practice as an example. In this book you have learned the proper setup, the back swing and the follow-through for that particular shot. Swing with deliberation and concentration, repeating every element with every swing until they have become second nature.

To practice without losing interest, you need a target to shoot for, a plan. Each session should include objectives. For instance, when you are practicing sand shots—exploding out of the trap—emulate Gary Player, a great sand shooter. Gary stayed at his sand-shot practices until he had holed out five shots.

You shouldn't expect that kind of perfection, but I do recommend that you give yourself a reasonable goal, say five shots that stop within three feet of the cup. Stick to it until you've achieved your goal or come close to it. Stress the target game.

With this kind of a plan for your practice, you will be able to see your improvement from week to week. Also it will expose your weaknesses right away.

Before beginning a practice session, hold a club or two behind your back and rotate the shoulders to stretch back muscles. Also warm up by swinging three clubs at once.

RECOMMENDED BREAKDOWN

Ideally, you may practice two or three times a week for 90 minutes per session. Based on this, I'm recommending that your sessions go something like this:

5 Minutes Warming Up—Loosen back muscles by twisting your torso gently. Swing with several clubs at once.

15 Minutes Pitching—Start with the pitching wedge. Review grip and setup. Try to achieve a balanced finish with easy swings. Pick out your target. Swing away and back at it. On the last 10 shots, really concentrate and see how accurate these shots are. Note how many have landed within five feet of the target. In your next session, again note how many of the last 10 are within five feet or better. See if you have improved.

When practicing with irons, try to achieve a good position at the top of the backswing. Check your shoulder turn and then the position of your hands.

15 Minutes with Middle Irons—Move on to the middle irons. Stress good backswing, coiling behind the ball. Achieve a balanced finish, while ending up facing the target. Note how accurately the last 10 shots are in achieving a straight line to the target.

15 Minutes with Woods—Hit several shots off the grass with the 4 or 5 wood. When you are satisfied, move on to your driver or 3 wood and tee up the ball to simulate course play. As before, check grip, setup, takeaway. Be sure you have coiled, turning away from the target. Use the last 10 shots to check how squarely you are putting the clubhead on the ball. This practice is helping you develop consistency

20 Minutes on Approaches—Even the pros occasionally miss when they hit to the green. A miss means having to hit an approach shot, usually from a difficult lie. This part of the practice will help give you a feel for the various lies—high grass, the slope toward the green, pitching over a trap, and so on.

With these shots, feel free to experiment with different irons. You might do better with a 7 than a 9 iron, or a pitching wedge over a 8. Look for situations that would be challenging out on the course. Set up balls on hard pan and shoot until you have confidence in this kind of "trouble" shot. Vary the distance from ball to green. Start at 30 feet and move up to 5 to 10 feet.

When practicing sand shots, draw a circle around the ball with a finger. Try to hit this circle of sand onto the green.

10 Minutes in Sand—Most players fear the sand. They shouldn't and wouldn't if they practiced hitting out of traps. End your practice time in the sand by seeing how many of the last 10 you can get up and down in two, if practical. The next session, compare and see what improvement has occurred. The point here is to strive for perfection. There's nothing more gratifying during a round than achieving a "sandy".

10 Minutes Putting—If you don't sink your putts, you don't score well, period! The two key elements in putting are distance and line. I recommend that you work on each aspect separately. Try these ideas in practice:

1) Draw a light line on the putting surface with a tee from the middle of the cup to the ball some five feet away. Be sure it is a level, straight-in putt. See how many in a row you can sink.

2) At six feet, see if you can drop five in a row. When you do, move back one or two feet and try again. Continue to move back until your percentages fall off.

3) Pick a spot some 25 feet from the cup. Work on judging the distance. Try to roll the ball about 12 inches *past* the cup. When your eye feels secure, go to an uphill putt. Then to a downhill putt. Hit the putt five times, holing out each time. See how often you are up and in in two. Make a note. The next session, see if you can do better.

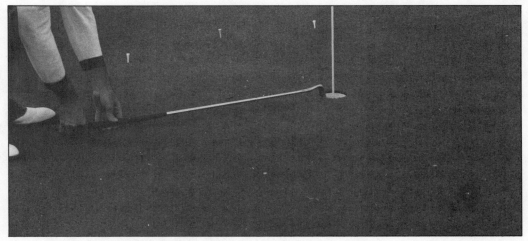

On long putts, use the first stroke to roll the ball within a circle of two feet or so. Use some tees to create this circle. Then putt until you can place five in a row inside this circle. Shrink the circle as your accuracy improves.

You also can use tees to create the proper clubhead path for a better putting stroke.

CHAPTER TWELVE

Important Rules To Know

The rules of golf are many, often misunderstood and confusing to the beginner. For these reasons, you should get the small paperback edition of the *Official USGA Rules of Golf* to carry in your bag. In addition, memorize the rules that most frequently come into play.

In this chapter, I've chosen those that should be memorized. Knowing these rules can help you avoid errors that in tournament play could cost you the match.

NUMBER OF CLUBS

We start with the fundamental, the number of clubs you can legally carry in your bag—14. The penalty is two strokes a hole, with a maximum penalty of four strokes. In match play the penalty is a loss of hole and a maximum of two holes lost.

THE BALL

The ball with which you play must meet USGA requirements in weight, size and initial velocity. To be on the safe side, use a nationally advertised brand or one approved by the USGA.

TEEING UP

On the tee, you must place the ball even with or behind the markers up to a limit of two club lengths. You cannot tee up the ball at any time in front of the markers. You may, however, stand outside the marker as long as the ball has been properly placed.

TEEING UP
This setup is completely legal.

BALL FALLING OFF THE TEE

If the ball falls off the tee during address, it can be replaced without penalty.

BALL MOVING

On the course, if the ball moves during address, there is a one-stroke penalty. It's your obligation to call this penalty on yourself.

STROKE

Any attempt to hit the ball is counted as a stroke, even if you miss it completely.

IMPEDIMENT

Any loose impediment lying on top, beside or under the ball may be removed without penalty, provided that the ball does not move. There is a one-stroke penalty if it does move. Removal is not allowed if the ball is in a hazard. However, if the ball is completely covered, you may, without penalty, remove enough of the impediment to locate the ball.

IMPROVING LIE

You are not permitted to improve your lie by moving, bending, or breaking anything that is alive and growing. In medal play, the penalty is two strokes; in match play, loss of hole.

IMPEDIMENT
Because this bough is dead, you can remove it. If it were alive, the rule on improving lie would be in force.

IMPEDIMENT
If the ball is buried in a hazard, you can partially uncover it without penalty.

PLAYING THE WRONG BALL

If the golfer mistakenly plays the wrong ball, the penalty is two strokes. In match play, it is loss of hole. If this occurs in partnership play, the golfer who plays the wrong ball is out of the hole. If his partner discovers the mistake before hitting and plays his own ball, he continues to be in competition on that hole. If he has hit the wrong ball himself, he also is out of the hole in match play and in stroke play, incurs a two-stroke penalty.

If the golfer is in stroke play, he must, when he discovers his wrong ball mistake, continue at that point to play on through the hole with his own ball, taking a two-stroke penalty. If he does not do so before playing from the next tee, he is disqualified.

The exception is if the golfer plays the wrong ball out of a hazard. He must, when the error is discovered, go back and play through with his own ball, without penalty. Strokes played with a wrong ball are not counted in the score.

OUT OF BOUNDS

Here's the most misunderstood element in this rule: When is the ball out? If any part of the ball is touching inside of the out-of-bounds marker, the ball is in play. The entire ball must be outside the marker line to be out of bounds. At that point, the player must go back to the spot where the shot originated and play again. The penalty is stroke and distance. That is, the golfer is now playing his third shot.

OUT OF BOUNDS
Here the ball is touching an out-of-bounds marker.

LOST BALL

The lost-ball penalty is the same as that for out of bounds—stroke and distance. It is important in helping to speed up play for the golfer who has hit an errant shot and fears he may have lost the ball to announce that he is hitting a *provisional*. Having hit a second ball, he has five minutes in which to search for the original ball. When hitting a provisional, it is advisable to make an identifying mark. This way, if you also hit the second astray, and if either ball is found, you can identify the ball.

LOST BALL
When you are going to hit a second ball, mark it.

HAZARD

The rule that determines whether a ball is in or out of bounds applies in reverse in determining whether a ball is in or out of a hazard. If any portion of the ball is even with the hazard marker, the ball is deemed to be within the hazard.

BALL DROP

Most golfers know that this rule has recently changed. Now when you are required to drop a ball—if you have been in a water hazard for instance—you are required to stand erect, hold the ball in your hand with the arm extended at shoulder length to make the drop.

BALL DROP
Here's how to do it.

You need not be facing the hole. If the ball accidentally touches player or equipment during or after the drop, you must drop again without penalty. If the ball rolls back into the hazard, you can drop again without penalty. If the second drop has the same result, you may place the ball by hand no nearer the hole without penalty and as close as possible to the spot where the ball first hit the ground.

UNPLAYABLE LIE

This rule is uncomplicated but often not fully understood. You may at any time declare a ball unplayable. You can then do any of the following: Take relief by dropping within two club lengths of the ball's resting place, no nearer the hole; go back in the line of flight as far back as you choose, keeping the stopping point of the ball between yourself and the hole; go back to the point where ball was hit and make the drop there. The penalty is the same for all three alternatives—one stroke.

STAKES

Different color stakes are used to mark the course. White stakes are out of bounds. Yellow stakes designate a water hazard. Lateral water hazards are marked by red stakes.

WATER HAZARD

If your ball goes into a water hazard, you may play it as it lies without penalty, being sure not to ground your club. If it can't be played, you have the options of first, dropping within two club lengths of the point of entry no nearer the hole; second, drop the ball behind the hazard keeping the spot where the ball last crossed the margin of the hazard between you and the hole; third, you may go back to the spot where you originally played the shot. All of these require a one-stroke penalty.

One aspect of dropping out from a water hazard that is often misunderstood: The drop occurs at the point where the ball in flight traverses the hazard, not at the point where the ball comes to rest.

LATERAL WATER HAZARD

A lateral water hazard gives the golfer whose ball has entered this hazard the choice of using all options of a water hazard and in addition, he may drop on the opposite side of the hazard with the same penalty, with the ball no closer to the hole and equidistant from the point of entry.

WATER HAZARD
Here, a ball was dropped behind the hazard.

SPECIAL COURSE CONDITIONS

The player whose ball comes to rest in an area marked as *ground under repair* may lift and drop without penalty. He also is granted relief if the ball comes to rest against or on an artificially constructed cart path. He gets relief as well if the ball lies in a hole made by a burrowing animal, unless this happens in a hazard.

PUTTING GREEN

Rules governing the putting green are many. Remember these in particular:

If putting or chipping from off the green, you can keep the flag stick in the cup and hit it with the ball without penalty.

If the stick is left in the cup and the ball is stroked from any portion of the green and hits the pin, there is a two-stroke penalty.

If, on the green and in stroke play, you strike your ball and it hits another ball, you suffer a two-stroke penalty.

The golfer on the putting green may not touch his club to the ground except to repair ball marks or old hole plugs. He may lift the ball on the green for the purpose of cleaning. The golfer may remove any loose impediment on the putting surface. In match play, the golfer may concede his opponent's putt at any time. There is no concession in stroke play.

The golfer may, while his ball is on the green, mark it and replace it when it is his turn to putt. He controls his ball at all times.

If the golfer's ball when hit lands on the wrong green, he is required to lift it and drop it away from the green, not nearer the hole, without penalty.

You must play the same ball until the hole is completed unless it becomes unfit for play. You may then announce that you are changing the ball to your playing partner and show him that it is not fit for play.

CONCLUSION

In conclusion, I'd like to relate an incident that took place early in my touring career. It was a Sunday evening and I had just finished playing a tournament in Milwaukee with undistinguished results. Julius Boros, an accomplished touring pro whose game and swing were the envy of everyone out there, accepted my offer of a ride to Chicago's O'Hare airport. On the ride I asked him if he had any secrets he'd be willing to part with.

He told me his own secret was visualization. He explained that whenever he was faced with a difficult shot he would visualize a time when he had previously executed just such a shot.

For example, if to get onto a green he was going to be forced to hit a low, hooking #5 iron 180 yards, he pictured a time in the past when he had actually hit such a shot. It might have been a shot from a tournament, a practice round or even on the practice range. But he visualized the entire successful sequence, from the moment of impact, through the low, curving plane, to seeing the ball land on target and roll towards the cup. Everything else he put out of his mind.

I thought about that and I thought about something else. Julie was leaving O'Hare on his way to Texas to play in the PGA Championship. I was on my way to play a satellite tournament in Waterloo, Iowa. I thought it just might be a good idea to listen to Mr. Boros. And that was the start of my thinking target golf—incorporating the positive approach discussed in this book.

Time after time a golfer will get into a groove on the practice range, sending shot after shot to the flag or some other specific target. Then this same golfer will leave the range, get to the first tee and make awful shots. He spends the rest of the day making swings to avoid trouble and gets nowhere.

I hope that won't ever happen to you (again). As this book emphasizes, the way to avoid trouble is not to look for it. Target your shots. Visualize where you want the ball to go. Play positive golf. You'll be amazed at the difference.

Oh, yes. I left that night with a new approach, a new attitude. And guess what? I tied for first in Waterloo. Julie? He won the PGA.

Index

Health, Fitness and Sports Books
from The Body Press

Fitness on the Road—Winsor	$7.95
High-Performance Racquetball—Hogan	8.95
Low-Stress Fitness—Brown	8.95
MuscleAerobics—Patano & Savage	8.95
Over the Hill—Kahn	8.95
Sports Injuries—Griffith	12.95
Super Soccer—Hudson/Herbst	7.95
Stretch & Relax—Tobias & Stewart	12.95
Symptoms, Illness & Surgery—Griffith	12.95
Target Golf—Pace/Barkow	7.95

The Body Press are available wherever fine books are sold, or order direct from the publisher. Send check or money order payable in U.S. funds to:

The Body Press, P.O. Box 5367, Dept. GLF-36, Tucson, AZ 85703

Include $1.95 postage and handling for first book; $1.00 for each additional book. Arizona residents add 7% sales tax. Please allow 4-6 weeks for delivery. Prices subject to change without notice.